INTRODUCTION TO VALUATION

Macmillan Building and Surveying Series

Series Editor: Ivor H. Seeley
Emeritus Professor, Nottingham Polytechnic

Advanced Building Measurement, second edition Ivor H. Seeley
Advanced Valuation Diane Butler and David Richmond
An Introduction to Building Services Christopher A. Howard
Applied Valuation Diane Butler
Asset Valuation Michael Rayner
Building Economics, third edition Ivor H. Seeley
Building Maintenance, second edition Ivor H. Seeley
Building Procurement Alan Turner
Building Quantities Explained, fourth edition Ivor H. Seeley
Building Surveys, Reports and Dilapidations Ivor H. Seeley
Building Technology, third edition Ivor H. Seeley
Civil Engineering Contract Administration and Control
    Ivor H. Seeley
Civil Engineering Quantities, fourth edition Ivor H. Seeley
Civil Engineering Specification, second edition Ivor H. Seeley
Computers and Quantity Surveyors Adrian Smith
Contract Planning and Contractual Procedures B. Cooke
Contract Planning Case Studies B. Cooke
Environmental Science in Building, second edition R. McMullan
Housing Associations Helen Cope
Introduction to Valuation D. Richmond
Principles of Property Investment and Pricing W.D. Fraser
Quality Assurance in Building Alan Griffith
Quantity Surveying Practice Ivor H. Seeley
Structural Detailing P. Newton
Urban Land Economics and Public Policy, fourth edition
    P.N. Balchin, J.L. Kieve and G.H. Bull
Urban Renewal Chris Couch
1980 JCT Standard Form of Building Contract, second edition
    R.F. Fellows

Other titles by the same authors

Housing Improvement and Social Inequality P.N. Balchin (Gower)
Housing Policy: An Introduction P.N. Balchin (Croom Helm)
Housing Policy and Housing Needs P.N. Balchin (Macmillan)
Regional and Urban Economics P.N. Balchin and G.H. Bull
    (Harper and Row)
The Electric Telegraph: An Economic and Social History J.L. Kieve
    (David and Charles)

INTRODUCTION TO VALUATION

SECOND EDITION

DAVID RICHMOND, F.R.I.C.S,F.S.V.A.

Principal Lecturer in Valuation,
Department of Surveying,
Trent Polytechnic,
Nottingham

MACMILLAN

First published 1975
Reprinted 1978, 1979, 1981, 1982, 1983
Second edition 1985
Reprinted 1989, 1990

Published by
MACMILLAN EDUCATION LTD
Houndmills, Basingstoke, Hampshire RG21 2XS
and London
Companies and representatives
throughout the world

Printed in Hong Kong

ISBN 0–333–38437–7

CONTENTS

PREFACE TO THE FIRST EDITION

The main purpose of this book is to assist those studying the subject of valuation for the Part 1 Examination of the Royal Institution of Chartered Surveyors and other relevant professional bodies, and for degrees and diplomas in estate management at universities and polytechnics. I also hope that it will be helpful to quantity, building and mineral surveying students, who require a knowledge of valuation in their studies, and others interested in the principles and techniques of property valuation.

Most examinations in valuation contain a number of questions involving calculations. In this connection the reader may benefit from attempting the questions included in chapters 3, 6, 7 and 8, the answers being provided at the end of the book. The chapter on mathematical aids should be of value for purposes of revision.

When answering questions with tax implications, the reader should apply the tax rates current at the time. I have used different tax rates throughout the book, so that the reader will appreciate that tax rates can vary according to the differing financial and personal circumstances of investors, and Finance Act changes.

I would like to express my thanks to Dr I. H. Seeley for his invaluable advice and encouragement; also to many other colleagues at Trent Polytechnic for their helpful comments.

Sincere thanks are also due to the Royal Institution of Chartered Surveyors and the Universities of London and Reading for permission to use past examination questions as examples and test questions.

Nottingham,   D. RICHMOND
Spring 1975

PREFACE TO THE SECOND EDITION

It is nine years since the First Edition of this book appeared, and during that time there has been considerable developments in valuation techniques and research.

In this edition I have taken out my original chapter on mathematical aids, due to the widespread use of calculators. I have updated the main text and extended chapter 5 (originally chapter 6) to take account of payments receivable other than annually in arrears.

Two new chapters have been produced on discounted cash flows and allowing for inflation and growth.

I have received helpful comments from both my students and my colleagues at Trent Polytechnic, for which I am very grateful. I would especially like to thank my 'partner' in valuation teaching, Neil Crosby, for his assistance in the preparation of chapter 9.

I would also like to thank Professor Ivor H. Seeley, the Series Editor, for his continued encouragement and assistance.

In the preface to the First Edition, I omitted to thank my mother for her help with proof-reading and indexing. I can now rectify this and thank her, rather belatedly!

Nottingham,
Spring 1984

DAVID RICHMOND

1 THE CONCEPT OF VALUATION

THE FUNCTION OF THE VALUER

The valuer is a member of the surveying profession who is primarily concerned with the valuation of land and/or buildings. Valuation may be defined as the estimation of the capital or rental value of land and/or buildings at a certain time. The valuer may also practise in estate agency, land economy, town and country planning or urban estate management.

An *estate agent* negotiates on behalf of clients the purchase, sale or lease of property; he may also arrange for the borrowing of capital by mortgage and advise on market and rental values of property. A *land economist* appraises the economic consequences of the use or development of land, taking into account financial and planning considerations. In *town and country planning*, the surveyor advises on all forms of land use and the economic problems and consequences appertaining to planning and development. The *urban estate manager* manages residential, commercial and industrial properties on behalf of the owners.

The valuer's special expertise, however, is to assess the capital or rental value of any particular property at a certain time. He will need to know the purpose for which the valuation is required and the intentions and circumstances of the client or employer on whose behalf it is being prepared. This information is essential, because it will affect the calculation of value. The valuation may be required for any of the following purposes.

The Purchase and Sale of Property

The valuer may represent either the prospective purchaser or the vendor. The price at which property is bought and sold may be established by private negotiation, tender or auction. The valuer representing the vendor may advertise that a property is for sale at a certain price and invite offers for its purchase. He will then negotiate with the prospective purchaser, who is the person to submit the most acceptable offer. The valuer may recommend the price at which the property should be offered.

Alternatively, property may be sold by tender; the vendor's valuer invites written offers to be submitted by a certain date. The vendor may then negotiate with the prospective purchaser, who is the person to submit the highest price.

A third method is to sell property by auction. The property is advertised for sale at a certain place and time. Bids for the purchase of the property are invited, and the offer by the bidder of the highest price may be accepted. However, prior to the auction, a reserve price may be fixed, that is, a price below which the property will not be sold.

The valuer who represents the vendor may recommend which method would be the most appropriate. He may take into account local and national circumstances. For example, a residential property may attract prospective purchasers from within the immediate locality only; however, there may be considerable local demand for this type of property, and the valuer may recommend a sale by private negotiation. Alternatively, he may feel that the demand would justify an auction sale. A commercial property having attractive investment possibilities may appeal to investors on a national scale, and the valuer may recommend sale by auction or tender.

The Letting of Property

The valuer may represent the owner of property — the landlord — who wishes to let it for the receipt of an annual sum (rent) or he may represent the tenant, who wishes to occupy the property for the payment of rent. In either case, the valuer may recommend to his client a price, which he considers to be the annual rental value of the property. He may also negotiate on behalf of his client the terms of the lease or tenancy agreement. If a landlord and tenant cannot agree the rent to be paid for the occupation of property, an independent valuer may be appointed to assess the rental value.

The Granting of Mortgage Facilities

A prospective purchaser of property may not have sufficient capital available to acquire the property, so that he may have to borrow money, which is to be repaid over a certain period of time. The amount may be borrowed by means of a mortgage, the property being regarded as a security. The valuer may represent a client who is lending capital, and he will value the property to ensure that it is worth the price that the purchaser is being asked to pay. (Mortgages are dealt with in chapters 2 and 5.)

Rating, Insurance, Taxation and other Specialised Purposes

The valuer may assess the value of property for specialised purposes such as rating assessments, payment of Capital Transfer Tax, taxation liabilities and insurance purposes.

The valuer may be employed in private practice, public service or be engaged on company work. The valuer employed in private practice with a professional firm may offer a service to all types of clients. The public service valuer may be employed by a government department, a nationalised industry or local government. The valuer engaged on company work may be employed by a property company, industrial or insurance group, or building society.

FACTORS AFFECTING THE VALUE OF PROPERTY

The value of an interest in property may be defined as the amount of money which can be obtained for that interest at a particular time from those who are able and willing to purchase it. A purchaser of an interest (legal estate) in property may buy for occupation, investment or speculation. Legal estates are considered in chapter 4. A purchaser for personal occupation will have regard to location and social and commercial facilities. In many instances the property will only attract a local market. A purchaser for investment purposes will consider the return he can obtain from the property in the form of rent, security and capital growth. (The calculations of value in this book are primarily for investment situations.) High-class investments frequently attract prospective purchasers on a national scale.

Speculators may purchase property with the hope of selling at a higher price in the future, thus making a capital gain. This type of activity may be curtailed by external restraints such as Income Tax and Capital Gains Tax liabilities.

In some transactions purchase of property may be for both occupation and investment. A prospective purchaser for investment purposes may compare property with other types of investment such as stocks and shares; these are considered in chapter 3. The valuer, when ascertaining value, must be aware of the economic and legal factors which affect both the existing and potential use of land and buildings; these are discussed in chapters 3 and 4.

Land is unique as an investment because it is naturally limited in supply. If there is considerable demand for manufactured products, the demand may be met by increasing the supply of those products. This is not so in the case of land, and it may be impractical to create additional land by schemes such as reclamation from the sea. If the supply of land cannot be equated with the demand for it, this will be reflected by increases in price.

The supply of land available for particular uses such as residential and commercial development is limited not only by natural factors such as location, topography and the load-bearing capacity of the ground but also by private and statutory factors. An owner of land or property may be restricted from using that land or property exactly as he wishes. This may be because at some time in the past, a condition has been imposed restricting the use of land or property, and it is still legally binding at the present time. Statutory control may, however, have a greater influence on the eventual use of land than private control. It is essential that, when the demand for land is increasing due to population growth, and improved living and technological standards, its eventual use should benefit as many people as possible. Successive governments have introduced legislation relating to the use and development of land and buildings in an attempt to make the best possible use of the land available.

Perhaps the most effective legislation is that relating to planning control, which is considered in detail in chapter 4. The local government authority dealing with planning (the local planning authority) has power to allocate the land in its administrative area for particular uses such as agricultural, residential or commercial. The authority also has the power to require an owner of land or buildings, who wishes to develop or change the use of that land or buildings, to obtain planning permission. An example will illustrate how these powers operate. An owner of land wishes to build a factory upon that land, and applies for planning permission. The land is allocated for residential development so the authority would normally refuse permission for industrial development but permit residential development.

For several years, the government has been concerned that certain investors and speculators have enjoyed considerable financial benefits from the disposal of property and the sale or renting of new developments. An attempt has been made to reduce these benefits by requiring the investor or speculator to pay Income Tax, Capital Gains Tax or Development Land Tax assessed on his gain. The rates at which taxes are paid may be altered according to economic circumstances. It is essential that the valuer knows the current tax rates when preparing a valuation.

The aim of the valuer is to assess market or rental value of property at a particular time, taking into account the factors previously discussed. Different valuers may, however, produce different values. They may have based their estimate of value upon prices obtained from similar transactions, and perhaps adjusted these values to take account of differences in the property. In many cases, these differences of opinion between valuers may be easily resolved by discussion or negotiation. However, in times of unstable market conditions, the valuer's task is made more difficult. Because the market value is dependent upon income to be received in the future, the valuer must attempt to anticipate future economic trends. This requires considerable skill and knowledge.

Valuation work also requires a certain amount of mathematical skill and the ability to set out calculations of value in a logical and comprehensible manner. The valuer may be required to justify his valuation to the Lands Tribunal (which consists of valuers and lawyers who are appointed to settle disputes relating to land and property), a local valuation court or other judicial and quasi-judicial proceedings.

THE PURPOSE OF VALUATION TABLES

To ascertain value, the valuer will need to possess certain numerical information such as the annual rent obtainable from the property and the return per annum which a purchaser could expect. This may be used mathematically to arrive at a figure of estimated value.

Example. Your client wishes to purchase a shop, which produces an annual income of £1000. Similar properties have recently yielded returns of 8 per cent per annum. Estimate the value of the property.

£1000 is 8 per cent of the capital value, hence

$$\text{the capital value} = £1000 \times \frac{100}{8}$$

$$= £1000 \times 12.5$$

$$= £12\ 500$$

The multiplier of 12.5 is termed the 'Years' Purchase' (YP).

The above example assumes that the annual income is perpetual. Many calculations will involve income which is receivable for limited periods only, and these calculations may be complex. The use of valuation tables saves time and may reduce mathematical error. There are several different types of valuation table, and their construction is considered in chapter 5 and their application to the calculation of values in chapters 6 and 7. The appropriate tables used in valuation are contained in Richard Parry, *Valuation Tables and Conversion Tables*, Estates Gazette, London (1978). In recent years, there have been other tables produced giving further information — P. Marshall, *Donaldsons Investment Tables*, Donaldsons (1979); J.J. Rose, *Rose's Property Valuation Tables*, The Freeland Press (1977); and P. Bowcock, *Property Valuation Tables*, Macmillan (1978).

2 THE MATHEMATICS OF VALUATION

The purpose of this chapter is to study the mathematics needed as a preliminary requisite to the solving of valuation problems in subsequent chapters.

The following abbreviations are extensively used

i = rate of interest per annum expressed as a decimal (rate of interest/100)

n = term of years (or the number of terms in a series)

ARITHMETICAL PROGRESSIONS

An arithmetical progression is a series of numbers, in which each term is formed from the preceding one by adding the same number to it. The amount to be added each time is termed the *common difference* and it may have a positive or a negative value.

The formula for calculating the sum of an arithmetical progression may be derived as follows.

Assume that an arithmetical progression has n terms, and that the first term is a and the common difference is d. The sequence of numbers emerges by adding d to the preceding number, and the series develops thus $a, a + d, a + 2d, a + 3d \ldots$ up to and including $a + (n - 1)d$ this being the last term. (The characteristic of d is one less than its place in the series, so that for the nth term, d has a characteristic of $n - 1$.)

It can be seen that the average of the first and last terms is the same as the average of the second and the next-to-last terms so that the average for the whole series is the average of the first and last terms, namely

$$\frac{a + (a + (n-1)d)}{2}$$

The sum of the arithmetical progression *Sn* is thus

$$Sn = \frac{n}{2}(a + a + (n-1)d)$$

$$= \frac{n}{2}(2a + (n-1)d)$$

Example. A man purchased a property last year, and during his first year of ownership has spent £150 on repairs. He anticipates that this amount will increase by £50 each year. What will be his total expenditure on repairs at the end of 14 years?

$$Sn = \frac{n}{2}(2a + (n-1)d)$$

where *Sn* = the total expenditure, *n* = 14, *a* = 150 and *d* = 50. Substituting in the formula

$$\text{Total expenditure} = \frac{14}{2}[(2 \times 150) + (13 \times 50)]$$

$$= 7 \times (300 + 650)$$

$$= 7 \times 950$$

$$= £6\,650$$

Example. Three consecutive numbers in an arithmetical progression have a total sum of 75 and a product of 15 000. Find the numbers.

Let the numbers be represented by $a - d$, a, $a + d$. Then

$$(a - d) + a + (a + d) = 75$$

$$3a = 75$$

$$a \text{ (the second term)} = 25$$

But

$$a(a-d)(a+d) = 15\,000$$

$$a(a^2 - d^2) = 15\,000$$

$$25(25^2 - d^2) = 15\,000$$

$$15\,625 - 25d^2 = 15\,000$$

$$d^2 = \frac{15\,625 - 15\,000}{25}$$

$$= \frac{625}{25} = 25$$

$$d = \pm 5$$

The three numbers are, therefore, 20, 25, and 30.

Example. The sum of the first nine terms of an arithmetical progression is 37.8 and the common difference is 0.2. Find the first term of the series.

$$Sn = \frac{n}{2}[2a + (n-1)d]$$

where $Sn = 37.8$, $n = 9$ and $d = 0.2$. Therefore

$$37.8 = \frac{9}{2}[2a + (8 \times 0.2)]$$

$$37.8 = 4.5(2a + 1.6)$$

$$37.8 = 9a + 7.2$$

$$9a = 30.6$$

$$a = \frac{30.6}{9}$$

$$= 3.4$$

GEOMETRICAL PROGRESSIONS

A geometrical progression is a series of numbers in which each term is formed from the preceding one by multiplying it by a constant factor, this factor being termed the *common ratio*.

The formula for calculating the sum of a geometrical progression may be derived as follows.

Assume that a geometrical progression has n terms, the first term is a and the common ratio is r. The standard form of a geometrical progression is

a, ar, ar^2, ar^3 ... up to and including ar^{n-1}

Let Sn = the sum of n terms

$$Sn = a + ar + ar^2 + ar^3 \text{ ... up to and including } ar^{n-2} + ar^{n-1} \quad (1)$$

Multiplying each term by r, gives

$$r\,Sn = ar + ar^2 + ar^3 + ar^4 \text{ ... up to and including } ar^{n-1} + ar^n \quad (2)$$

Subtracting equation 1 from equation 2 gives

$$r\,Sn - Sn = ar^n - a$$
$$Sn(r - 1) = a(r^n - 1)$$
$$Sn = \frac{a(r^n - 1)}{r - 1}$$

If r has a negative value or is a fraction less than unity, the formula is reversed thus

$$Sn = \frac{a(1 - r^n)}{1 - r}$$

Example. A property owner estimates that his repair costs will increase by 11 per cent each year. What will be the total cost of repairs at the end of 12 years, if his first year costs are £120?

In the geometrical progression formula

$$Sn = \frac{a(r^n - 1)}{r - 1}$$

Sn = total expenditure, $a = 120$

$r = 1.11$ and $n = 12$

Thus total expenditure $= \dfrac{120(1.11^{12} - 1)}{1.11 - 1}$

$$= \dfrac{120(3.496 - 1)}{0.11}$$

$$= £2\,723$$

Example. Find the ninth term of the series $+ 2, - 4, + 8, - 16, \ldots$

In this series $a = 2$ and $r = -2$. Hence the ninth term is

$$ar^{9-1} = 2 \times (-2)^8$$

$$= 2 \times 256$$

$$= + 512$$

SIMPLE INTEREST

If money is loaned or invested the owner of that money will expect a return for having foregone an alternative use of these funds. This return is generally in the form of interest, which will accumulate at regular intervals, usually on an annual basis. The interest may be paid to the owner at regular intervals, and does not then itself accumulate interest. This is simple interest. The following example shows how simple interest is calculated.

Example. Calculate the simple interest on £70 for 3½ years at 9 per cent.

Interest on £1 for 1 year is £0.09

Interest on £70 for 1 year is £(70×0.09)

Interest on £70 for 3½ years is £$(70 \times 0.09 \times 3.50)$

$$= £22.05$$

Thus in general terms, if

P = the principal amount

i = rate of interest per annum expressed as a decimal

n = term of years

and I = total simple interest

then $I = P \times i \times n$

The reader may be acquainted with an alternative formula

$$I = \frac{P \times R \times T}{100}$$

where R = rate of interest per annum and T = term of years.

To calculate the total amount of original capital and interest, the principal amount is added to the total simple interest $(P + I)$.

The formula may be transposed to find the principal amount, the rate of interest per annum or the term of years. Thus

$$P = \frac{I}{i \times n}$$

$$i = \frac{I}{P \times n}$$

and

$$n = \frac{I}{P \times i}$$

Example. Calculate the amount which will have accumulated at the end of 5 years from a loan of £840 at 4½ per cent simple interest.

In this example, P = £840, i = 0.045 and n = 5 years.

$$\begin{aligned}
\text{Amount accumulated} &= P + I \\
&= P + (P \times i \times n) \\
&= 840 + (840 \times 0.045 \times 5) \\
&= 840 + 189 \\
&= £1029
\end{aligned}$$

Example. What sum would have to be invested at 9 per cent per annum rate of interest to provide an income of £500 per annum?

$i = 0.09$, $n = 1$ year and $I = £500$.

$$P = \frac{I}{i \times n}$$

$$= \frac{500}{0.09 \times 1}$$

$$= £5556$$

Example. Find the operative rate of simple interest per annum if £700 accumulates to £950 after 4 years.

$I = £950 - £700 = £250$, $P = £700$ and $n = 4$ years.

$$i = \frac{I}{P \times n}$$

$$= \frac{250}{700 \times 4}$$

$$= \frac{250}{2\,800}$$

$$= 0.089$$

$$= 9 \text{ per cent (approximately)}$$

Example. How many years does it take a sum of money to increase by 75 per cent when the rate of simple interest is 7½ per cent per annum?

$I = 0.75P$ and $i = 0.075$.

$$n = \frac{I}{P \times i}$$

If $P = £1$, then

$$n = \frac{0.75}{1 \times 0.075}$$

$$= 10 \text{ years}$$

COMPOUND INTEREST

As previously stated, where money is invested, the investor will expect an annual return, that is, a rate of interest per annum. Instead of receiving a monetary return at regular intervals, he may choose to have the interest added to the principal amount. This interest, which will also accumulate further interest, is termed *compound interest*. A formula may be derived as follows.

Assume £1 is invested at i compound interest. At the end of the first year, £1 will accumulate to $(1 + i)$. At the end of the second year, it will accumulate to $(1 + i)i + (1 + i) = 1 + 2i + i^2 = (1 + i)^2$. At the end of the third year the sum will further accumulate to $(1 + 2i + i^2)i + (1 + 2i + i^2) = 1 + 3i + 3i^2 + i^3 = (1 + i)^3$. So that at the end of n years, £1 will have accumulated to $£(1 + i)^n$. Thus

$$\text{total amount accumulated} = £(1 + i)^n$$

and $\quad\quad$ total interest $\quad\quad\quad\quad\quad = £(1 + i)^n - 1$

For the investment of a principal amount P and the total amount A

$$A = P(1 + i)^n$$

Example. To what amount will £750 accumulate after 5 years at 8½ per cent compound interest?

P = £750, n = 5 years and i = 0.085.

$$A = P(1 + i)^n$$

$$A = 750 \times 1.085^5$$

$$= 750 \times 1.503$$

$$= £1\,127$$

The formula may be transposed to find the principal amount, the rate of interest per annum or term of years. Thus

$$P = \frac{A}{(1 + i)^n}$$

$$i = \sqrt[n]{\frac{A}{P}} - 1$$

and

$$n = \frac{\log A - \log P}{\log (1 + i)}$$

Example. A man aged 57 years wishes to obtain a capital sum of £2 000 on retirement in 8 years' time. What sum must he invest now at 9 per cent compound interest?

A = £2 000, n = 8 years and i = 0.09.

$$P = \frac{A}{(1 + i)^n}$$

$$= \frac{2\,000}{1.09^8}$$

$$= \frac{2\,000}{1.993}$$

$$= £1004$$

Example. An investor wishes to double his capital after a period of 10 years. At what rate of compound interest per annum would he need to invest to achieve this?

$$A = 2P \text{ and } n = 10 \text{ years}$$

$$i = \sqrt[n]{\frac{A}{P}} - 1$$

$$= \sqrt[10]{\frac{2}{1}} - 1$$

$$= 1.072 - 1$$

$$= 0.072$$

$$= 7.2 \text{ per cent}$$

Example. A man has invested £1 200 at 8½ per cent compound interest. How long will it take for this amount to accumulate to £2 000?

A = £2000, P = £1200 and i = 0.085.

$$n = \frac{\log A - \log P}{\log (1 + i)}$$

$$= \frac{\log 2000 - \log 1200}{\log 1.085}$$

$$= \frac{3.3010 - 3.0792}{0.0354}$$

$$= \frac{0.2218}{0.0354}$$

$$= 6.26 \text{ years}$$

MORTGAGE REPAYMENTS

If a capital sum of money is borrowed over a period of time, the lender may stipulate that repayment should be made at regular intervals during the period of borrowing, each repayment being of an equal amount. The agreement to lend and borrow capital for the purchase of land and/or property may be termed a *mortgage*; the borrower is called the *mortgagor*, and the lender the *mortgagee*.

Let the amount of the mortgage be M, and the annual repayments be P. If the mortgagee lends M for a period of n years, he releases not only M, but also the compound interest, at an annual rate of i, which would otherwise have accumulated each year; the total thus being $M(1 + i)^n$. The annual repayments P will also be able to accumulate compound interest at an annual rate of i.

The first payment of P will accumulate to $P(1 + i)^{n-1}$, the second payment of P to $P(1 + i)^{n-2}$, and so on. The sum of the repayments and interest will be $P(1 + i)^{n-1} + P(1 + i)^{n-2}$ and ...up to and including $P(1 + i)^2 + P(1 + i) + P$. If this is reversed, the sum of repayments and interest $= P + P(1 + i) + P(1 + i)^2$ ... up to and including $P(1 + i)^{n-2} + P(1 + i)^{n-1}$.

This is a geometrical progression; the formula for the sum, proved earlier in this chapter, is

$$Sn = \frac{a(r^n - 1)}{r - 1}$$

where

Sn = the sum of repayments and interest

$a = P$

$r = (1 + i)$

Hence the sum of repayments and interest is

$$P\left[\frac{(1+i)^n - 1}{(1+i) - 1}\right]$$

$$= P\left[\frac{(1+i)^n - 1}{i}\right]$$

The total of repayments and interest must equal the value of the mortgage with its interest. Thus

$$\frac{P((1+i)^n - 1)}{i} = M(1+i)^n$$

So

$$P = \frac{M(1+i)^n i}{(1+i)^n - 1}$$

Example. What would be the annual repayments on a mortgage of £4500 borrowed over 25 years at 11 per cent compound interest?

$$P = \frac{M(1+i)^n i}{(1+i)^n - 1}$$

where M = £4500, i = 0.11 and n = 25 years.

$$P = \frac{4500 \times 1.11^{25} \times 0.11}{1.11^{25} - 1}$$

$$= \frac{4500 \times 13.57 \times 0.11}{13.57 - 1}$$

$$= \frac{6716}{12.57}$$

$$= £534.3$$

A mortgagor may decide that there is a maximum amount he can afford to pay in annual repayments, and he will wish to know the maximum amount, M, that he will be able to borrow. This can be found by transposing the formula

$$M = \frac{P((1 + i)^n - 1)}{(1 + i)^n \, i}$$

Example. A prospective mortgagor calculates that he can afford repayments totalling £250 per annum over a period of 25 years. If the borrowing rate is 10 per cent per annum, what is the maximum amount he can borrow?

$$M = \frac{P((1 + i)^n - 1)}{(1 + i)^n \, i}$$

P = £250, i = 0.10 and n = 25 years. Thus

$$M = \frac{250 \times (1.10^{25} - 1)}{1.10^{25} \times 0.10}$$

$$= \frac{250 \times 9.84}{10.84 \times 0.10}$$

$$= \frac{2460}{1.084}$$

$$= £\,2270$$

Mortgages will be considered further in chapter 5 when a mortgage instalment table will be analysed.

DEPRECIATION

When new plant or machinery is purchased, its value as at purchase will depreciate year by year. This annual depreciation may be expressed as a fixed percentage, i, per annum, when the value at any particular time can be determined by means of a compound interest calculation with a negative value. Thus, if the original value = P, the depreciating rate of interest per annum = i, term of years = n and the value after n years = D, then

$$D = P(1 - i)^n$$

Example. At the end of each year the depreciation of certain plant is taken as 8 per cent of its value at the beginning of the year. If the initial value is £3 000, calculate the value after 7 years.

P = £3000, i = 0.08 and n = 7 years.

$$D = 3000 (1 - 0.08)^7$$

$$= 3000 \times 0.92^7$$

$$= £1674$$

Example. Equipment costs £500 when new. It is estimated that it depreciates in value by 10 per cent each year. In how many years (to the nearest year) will it be reduced to scrap value of £5?

P = £500, D = £5 and i = 0.10.

$$D = P(1 - i)^n$$

$$5 = 500(1 - 0.10)^n$$

$$5 = 500 \times 0.90^n$$

$$0.90^n = 0.01$$

$$\log 0.90 \times n = \log 0.01$$

$$n = \frac{\log 0.01}{\log 0.90} = \frac{\bar{2}.0000}{\bar{1}.9542}$$

$$= \frac{-2}{-1 + 0.9542}$$

$$= \frac{-2}{-0.0458}$$

$$= 44 \text{ years}$$

QUESTIONS

2.1 What sum would have to be invested at 11 per cent per annum simple interest to provide an annual income of £750?

2.2 How many years will it take a sum of money to double itself when the rate of simple interest is 9 per cent per annum?

2.3   A man invests £250 at 9½ per cent compound interest. To what amount will this accumulate at the end of 15 years?

2.4   A man wishes to provide a capital sum of £1500 in 10 years' time. What must he invest now if the compound interest rate is 8½ per cent per annum?

2.5   An investor wishes to treble his capital over a period of 9 years. What rate of compound interest per annum would he require to achieve this?

2.6   Find the sum of the series $8 + 7.75 + 7.50 + \ldots + 0.25 + 0$.

2.7   Three numbers in an arithmetical progression have a product of 280 and a sum of 21. Find the numbers.

2.8   Find the sum of the first ten terms of the series $+12 - 6 + 3 \ldots$.

2.9   What will be the annual repayments on a debt of £4000 borrowed over 30 years, if the compound interest rate is 8 per cent per annum?

2.10 A man wishes to borrow a capital sum but the maximum annual repayment he can afford to make over a 35 year period is £400. If the borrowing rate is 9 per cent per annum, what is the maximum amount he can borrow?

2.11 A builder buys a machine for £1000 and calculates depreciation at the rate of 13 per cent each year. In how many years will the machine be reduced to scrap value of £35?

2.12 A piece of machinery costs £1200 when new. It is estimated that it depreciates by 12 per cent per annum for the first three years and 10 per cent thereafter. What will be its value at the end of 10 years?

3 PRINCIPLES AND SOURCES OF INVESTMENT

The essential nature of any investment is the forgoing of a capital sum in return for a regular income over a period of time. A person who has capital surplus to his immediate requirements may retain this for future contingencies. However, a better alternative would be to put his capital to work by investing it and enjoying a return of income, probably on an annual basis.

The prudent investor will consider the alternative types of investment available to him by comparing each with the 'ideal investment'. This has four qualities

(i) Security of capital in relation to ease of withdrawal. The investor may, at some future date, need to transfer his investment back into cash at short notice. It is thus essential that the investment can be sold for, or converted to, cash at any particular time.

(ii) Security of income in relation to purchasing power. The investor will wish to ensure that the regular or annual income can be maintained in the future. He would also hope that the income would increase sufficiently in the future to counteract inflationary trends.

(iii) Minimum inconvenience and expense in management. Investments may vary in the amount of inconvenience and cost of collecting or obtaining the income.

(iv) Minimum of inconvenience and expense in selling. Investments in banks and building societies may be easily and cheaply converted into cash, whereas conversion of those in land and property will prove to be more costly and time-consuming.

The investor will also consider the yield given by each of his alternative investment outlets. The yield is the relationship between the capital paid for the investment and the income which derives from it.

Example. A man invests £1000 in a deposit account in a bank. His annual interest or return is £90. The yield is 90/1000 × 100 = 9 per cent.

If the ideal investment with the four desirable qualities did exist, the investor would merely require a fee for the use of his money. In practice, however, investments will differ in the extent to which they possess these four qualities, and these differences will cause a varying pattern of yields. If one investment appears to involve greater risk than another, then the investor will expect a greater return or reward. Hence, the lower the ratio of risk to capital and income, the smaller will be the yield.

THE INVESTMENT MARKET

Some holders of surplus cash will purchase investments, and at any given time there will be a stock of investments in existence. Some investors may wish to turn their investments back into cash and, conversely, some holding cash may wish to invest it.

The function of the investment market is to equate these two opposing activities. If the supply of an investment at a particular time is greater than the demand for it at the prevailing price, then the price will fall and the yield will rise in consequence. This will probably stimulate increased demand, because of the improved yield. It might also have the effect of reducing the supply of investments available for purchase because the lower price would deter existing owners of those investments from selling. This process would continue until supply and demand became equal. At a time of economic uncertainty, there may be a tendency to retain surplus capital rather than invest it. This may result in depressed prices and enhanced interest rates. The level of interest rates will also be influenced by the Minimum Lending Rate (formerly the Bank Rate) operated by the Bank of England.

SOURCES OF INVESTMENT

The investor may have a number of alternative sources available to him, such as

    (i)   banks and building societies
    (ii) stocks and shares
    (iii) unit trusts
    (iv) land and property

Banks and Building Societies

Investment in the deposit account of a bank will compare favourably with the ideal investment since invested capital is quickly and cheaply recouped if required. The income (interest) is safe and is added to the invested amount at regular intervals. The sum of a bank's capital investments will influence the amount that it will be able to lend. Lending may take the form of either an overdraft or a personal loan. An overdraft is not a personal right and it must be adequately backed with security for the loan required. The security must have a greater value than the amount to be borrowed, and banks favour securities such as property and stocks and shares which can be readily realised.

A personal loan does not require security and could be regarded as an alternative to hire purchase. A sum is borrowed for a specific purpose on the basis of monthly repayments with interest; this interest being paid on the original loan and not the declining balance owed.

Building societies have many of the desirable qualities attributable to investments with the banks. Both capital and income are secure, and the building society attempts to cater for a wide range of investors. Sums may be deposited by an investor at any time, although the regular saver may undertake to invest an agreed amount at fixed intervals, often monthly, and in return the building society pays a higher rate of interest.

The availability of capital for borrowers is directly influenced by the total amount of investment in the building society. The lending of capital is normally undertaken by means of a mortgage. The building society will need to consider the age, personal circumstances and earning capacity of prospective borrowers, in order to calculate the maximum amount to be lent over an agreed period, as well as the security that the property affords.

Small investors might favour the National Savings Bank or National Savings Certificates as their investment outlet.

Stocks and Shares

As an alternative to investment in banks or building societies, an investor may consider stocks and shares, which are normally bought and sold on the Stock Exchange.

In the past, enterprises needing capital for such varied purposes as the formation of business, purchase of land or expansion plans, found that they could not always borrow from their circle of acquaintances. It was also impractical to pay on demand to any lender who wanted his capital returned, because the money had been used for some permanent venture. To raise large amounts of capital, joint stock companies were established; the capital of these companies came from large numbers of investors, who bought shares in the companies. This system is still in existence. If an investor wishes to redeem his capital, he may sell his shares through the Stock Exchange. The Stock Exchange operates as a market place, where buyers and sellers are brought together to sell or buy shares at prices which are determined by the free competition of the open market. Government and local authorities, as well as industrial and commercial concerns, raise capital through the medium of the Stock Exchange.

The Stock Exchange has been in existence since the seventeenth century, and guards its good reputation by enforcing strict conditions and qualifications upon members seeking election. The London Stock Exchange has 3500 members, consisting of brokers and jobbers. Brokers deal with the public, who are their clients, buying and selling shares as instructed. Jobbers have no direct contact with the public; they are wholesalers dealing in stocks and shares and probably specialising in different groups of securities. The jobber 'makes a price' (really two prices — one, the lower, at which he will buy and the other, the higher, at which he will sell). The margin between the two prices (known as 'the jobber's turn') represents the jobber's profit. It is the duty of the broker, in negotiating with jobbers, to obtain the best possible deal on behalf of his client. There are Associated Stock Exchanges in the provinces, European Stock Exchanges and overseas branches. The main types of stocks and shares are

Fixed-interest Securities. An investor will be attracted to these, when he wishes to ensure that his income and capital will be certain. The security quotes a specific return upon the face value. For example, a 5 per cent £1 share will yield a return of 5p each year. The disadvantage of this type of investment is that it may fail to keep pace with inflationary trends; there is no guarantee that income will have the same purchasing power as at present.

Capital required in the public sector may be raised by this type of investment, examples being short-term Local Government loans and Defence Bonds.

Ordinary Shares or Equities. The return on these investments is dependent on the profits a company makes, and may, accordingly, vary from year to year. The possibility of both risk and reward is greater than with the fixed-interest security, so that care needs to be taken in both choice and timing.

In choosing a suitable investment, the likely rate of growth will be important. This may be judged on the past performance of the industry to which the company belongs, and whether or not the company would be responsive and prepared for technological changes.

Preference Shares. These are fixed-dividend shares in joint stock companies, the dividend being paid before ordinary shares. If a company cannot pay at a particular time, its responsibility to do so remains. The interest is cumulative and past arrears of preference interest must be paid before there can be any dividend on the rest of the capital.

Debenture Stocks or Bonds. These are not shares in a business, but loans which create a right to a fixed rate of interest. Holders are entitled to receive their interest before payment of dividends on ordinary shares. Government and public authorities may also borrow money by means of fixed loans which are repayable after a given number of years. These can be bought and sold for their current market value on the Stock Exchange.

Unit Trusts

Unit trusts came into existence in order to reduce the risks to the ordinary investor by giving him the opportunity to spread his investment over a number of companies. There are two independent organisations involved in the formation of a unit trust — a trustee and a management company. The trustee, usually a bank, looks after cash and securities, and ensures that an adequate reserve fund is established, while the management company is responsible for the choice of individual securities. At regular intervals the managers value the securities in the trust and divide the total by the number of units in issue, and in this way values are determined for buying and selling.

Land and Property

Land and property will be considered for investment purposes in chapter 4.

YIELD AND DIVIDEND

As stocks and shares are bought and sold, their market value may vary from their original value (nominal value) when issued. A fixed-interest security will have a stated dividend, which may differ from the yield. For example, if a company issued £1 shares yielding a 5 per cent dividend and their market value subsequently increased to £2, then the yield would be 5p on a purchase price of £2, that is, 2½ per cent. Hence

$$\text{Yield} = \frac{\text{nominal value} \times \text{dividend}}{\text{market value}}$$

Comparisons of both yield and security will influence the investor as to his ultimate choice for capital outlay.

4 LAND AND PROPERTY AS AN INVESTMENT

In legal terms, 'land' means the topsoil and all the strata below and the air space above. If a building or roads or paths are constructed upon land, they become part of the land, although it is common practice to refer to 'land and buildings'. The term 'real property' is also used to signify 'land and buildings'.

Real property as a medium for investment differs considerably in its qualities and characteristics compared with the other investment outlets previously mentioned. It is naturally limited in supply and it would be extremely difficult and expensive to create additional land to meet expanding requirements. No two pieces of land are exactly alike in every respect. They will differ in size, topography, locality and condition.

Real property will not be available in regular units for investment as are stocks and shares, (there is no equivalent to the £1 share). The size of the investment in the real property market may be such that, generally, it will exclude the small investor unless he wishes to invest in property bonds. To acquire real property the prospective purchaser must usually be considering market values of property units in terms of thousands of pounds, not in tens or hundreds of pounds. Because this type of investment is on a large-scale basis it is regarded favourably by investors such as pension funds and insurance companies, who have large funds available for investment.

LEGAL ESTATES

A special characteristic of land and buildings is that a piece of land or a building may have legal estates existing in it which are capable of being purchased and sold in the open market. The legal system of land ownership has developed from olden times, but was simplified by the Law of Property Act 1925 which provided two legal estates in land, 'the tenancy in fee simple' and 'the term certain'.

The tenancy in fee simple (or 'the fee simple absolute in possession') is popularly called the freehold. This is the superior interest in land, being perpetual, that is, of an endless period of time. The owner of such an estate has the right to occupy, enjoy and dispose of his property should he so wish, subject to certain limitations to be considered later in this chapter. If he still owns the property on death, it forms part of his estate.

The term certain (or 'the term of years absolute in possession') is popularly called the leasehold. This is created for a specific period of time, such as weekly, monthly, annually or a definite number of years, and gives the leaseholder (or the *lessee* or *tenant*) the right to occupy and enjoy the property over that period of time. He will usually pay rent to the landlord for the benefit of his occupation. Theoretically, at the end of the lease the landlord will be entitled to the property free from the tenant's rights, and he is thus said to own the reversion in the property. In certain cases, however, the tenant may obtain an extension of the period of the lease and continue his occupation. This will occur in the case of certain business tenancies under the Landlord and Tenant Act 1954, and agricultural properties under the Agricultural Holdings Act 1948. Similarly, in certain residential tenancies under Part 1, the Landlord and Tenant Act 1954 and Rent Acts 1965-77, the tenant may have the right to stay in possession. Under the Leasehold Reform Act 1967, the tenants of residential properties under ground leases may purchase the freehold at any time during the unexpired period of the lease if they satisfy certain requirements.

A tenant may decide that he no longer wishes to occupy the land or property, and he may either 'sublet' or 'assign' the land or property. The lease may require the tenant to obtain the landlord's permission to sublet or assign.

Where the tenant sublets, he grants occupation for a period less than his own, and the new occupant is termed the *sublessee* or *underlessee*; the original lessee under this arrangement may be termed the *sublessor* or *underlessor*. The original lessee (head lessee) will still be responsible to the freeholder for conditions imposed in the lease. Likewise, the sublessee will be responsible to his landlord, the head lessee, for conditions imposed in the sublease; these conditions may be different from those of the head lease.

An assignment differs from a sublease in that the lessee, with his landlord's permission, transfers all his rights to the *assignee* for the full residue of the term. The assignee is thus responsible to the freeholder for satisfying conditions imposed in the original lease.

The lease is an agreement under seal by which a tenancy is granted by a landlord (the lessor) to a tenant (the lessee). If the agreement is executed under hand (written but not under seal), it is termed a *tenancy agreement*, and if created orally it is termed an *oral agreement*. Leases granted for a term of more than three years must be under seal. The lease should state the term of the lease, specify the amount of rent per annum to be paid, when it is to be paid and at what intervals (if any) it will be reviewed. The lease should also state the division of responsibility for repairs and insurance.

In a full repairing and insuring lease the tenant will be responsible for carrying out all repairs and insurance, whereas in an internal repairing lease the tenant will be responsible for internal repairs only, the landlord retaining responsibility for external repairs and insurance.

Where a freeholder grants a lease of building land to a lessee for a long period, such as 99 years, this may be termed a *ground lease*. The rent paid (a ground rent) will be for the use of the land only, and the lessee may erect buildings upon the land for his own occupation or for subletting. At the end of the ground lease, both the land and the buildings upon it will revert to the freeholder, except in certain cases involving residential property, where a lessee may have a right to purchase the freehold interest under the Leasehold Reform Act 1967. (The lessee is given the right to purchase the freehold at any time during the unexpired term of the lease.)

If a lease is granted for the occupation of land and/or buildings, it may be termed an *occupation lease*. If the tenant pays the full rental value of the property this is known as a *rack rent*. (In the case of a full repairing and insuring lease, it may be termed a *net rack rent*.) If, however, the rent paid by the lessee is less than full rental value it is a *head rent* and the lessee enjoys a *profit rent*, that is, the difference between the full rental value (the rack rent) and the rent actually paid (the head rent).

Equitable Interests

There may exist also, in real property, *equitable interests* such as the *tenancy in fee tail* and the *tenancy for life*. These interests are created so that property is settled on a person for life and after his death passes to his eldest son and the heirs of his body. The interest may thus pass from generation to generation unless there are no heirs (in which case the interest reverts to the heirs of the original grantor), or the entail is barred. Under the Settled Land Act 1925, a tenant for life may bar the entail by selling the interest in the settled property, the capital money being paid to the trustees and settled to the same uses as was the land itself.

CONTROLS ON LAND USAGE

A freeholder or lessee may be restricted from using land or property exactly as he wishes, because he may be subjected to private and/or statutory controls.

Private Control

Private control on land usage may take the form of restrictive covenants, easements and profits *à prendre*, and licences and wayleaves.

Restrictive covenants are agreements restricting the users of freehold land, which are enforceable not only between the original contracting parties, but also between subsequent successors of those parties. If an owner wishes to sell some of his land, he may continue to live nearby. He may thus impose conditions on the purchaser of the land so as to protect himself as to amenity and privacy, and to maintain the market value of the land he retains. Typical examples of a restrictive covenant would be conditions as to a maximum number and the type of building(s) to be erected on the land and obligations such as fencing or tree-planting requirements. A developer, when selling houses on an estate may require purchasers to comply with certain obligations, such as the type of fencing to be erected, with a view to maintaining certain minimum standards.

As time passes, it may appear that the restrictive covenant no longer enhances the value of the benefited property, because the surrounding area has altered in character. The covenant may be discharged or modified by agreement of the parties concerned or by application to the Lands Tribunal. The Lands Tribunal may discharge or modify a restrictive covenant if it is considered to be obsolete, or if it prevents the reasonable use of the land for public or private purposes. Or it may be that the discharge or modification would not injure those who benefit from the restriction. If, however, the person who benefits from the restriction would suffer from the discharge or modification, then the landowner will be ordered to pay him compensation.

An easement is a privilege (without the right to take anything from the soil) which the owner of one piece of land, the dominant tenement, has over the other, the servient tenement, to compel its owner to permit something to be done or to refrain from doing something on the servient tenement, for the benefit of the owner of the dominant tenement. Examples are

    (i) Rights of way. A freeholder may have a right to pass over an adjoining owner's land in order to gain access to his own land.

    (ii) A freeholder may be prevented from building on his land in a position that will reduce the access of light to the windows of a property on adjoining land.

A profit *à prendre* is a right to take something from another person's land, such as the soil, natural produce of the land or wild animals existing on it, (but a right to take water from a pump or spring is an easement). Easements and profits may be created in the following ways.

    (i) Statute. They are frequently created by local Acts of Parliament.

    (ii) Express Grant. The express granting of easements and profits may occur between neighbouring owners, such as rights of access and permission to lay a drain over land owned by a neighbour.

    (iii) Implied Grant and Long User. When a landowner sells part of his land, certain easements over the land retained are implied in favour of the grantee. Section 62 of the Law of Property Act 1925 deems the items which shall pass with land when it is conveyed, and it may transfer or create such easements as rights of way and rights of light. To avoid this, the vendor may have to incorporate in his conveyance express exclusion of these rights.

If a lawful right has been enjoyed over a long period of time, even though no evidence of its actual grant can be produced, the court will uphold the right assuming it to have a lawful origin. This is termed 'prescription' and may be acquired at common law, by lost modern grant or under the Prescription Act 1832.

At common law, an owner may attempt to show that the usage existed since time immemorial, that is, since 1189 (known as 'prescription at common law'). This is difficult to establish, so that a court may presume that a grant was made subsequent to 1189 but has since been lost (known as 'lost modern grant'). The court may presume a right if 20 years' usage can be shown. The Prescription Act 1832 was passed to overcome difficulties experienced by prescribing at common law or under the doctrine of lost modern grant.

In the case of profits, a claim cannot be defeated on the grounds that the usage commenced after 1189 if 30 years' uninterrupted enjoyment can be proved. If 60 years' uninterrupted enjoyment can be shown, the right becomes absolute unless enjoyed by written consent. The same rule applies to easements, other than those relating to light, except that the respective time periods are 20 and 40 years. Where the access to and use of light by any building has been enjoyed without interruption for 20 years, the right becomes absolute unless it was enjoyed by a consent or agreement in writing.

Easements and profits may be extinguished by statute or release by the dominant tenement. An owner may find that if a way over his land has been used by the public without interruption for a period of 20 years, then it may be deemed to be dedicated as a highway. To prevent this, he must show that he has no intention of dedicating the land as a public highway. This may be achieved by erecting a notice on the land, giving a notice to the appropriate local authority, or closing for one day a year.

Licences and wayleaves are created by statute or with the consent of the landowner. These are rights to enter on another's land for the purposes of erecting, constructing and maintaining works on that land. Annual payments may be made for these rights. Examples are the laying of telephone cables, erection of electric power pylons, traffic signs and advertisements. The written agreement usually provides a period of notice to be given by either party for the extinguishment of the right.

STATUTORY CONTROLS

Planning Control

Many owners may feel that their land could be used for an alternative purpose, which would make it more valuable, such as residential development on agricultural land. However, they may be restricted by planning control. The present system of planning control originated with the Town and Country Planning Act 1947, which created local planning authorities to prepare plans and control development. Since April 1974, the responsibility for planning may be shared by county and district councils. Under the 1947 Act, local planning authorities were required to prepare development plans for their administrative areas. These plans allocated land for different uses, such as residential, shopping, industrial and roads. They also indicated areas requiring development or redevelopment and designated land subject to acquisition by compulsory purchase.

A new system was introduced by the Town and Country Planning Acts 1968 and 1971, which required local planning authorities to prepare structure and local plans. The local planning authority, after carrying out a survey of its administrative area, prepares a structure plan, which is constantly revised. This plan formulates the local planning authority's policy and general proposals in respect of the development and other use of land in its area. It will include measures for the improvement of the physical environment and management of traffic. The plan should also state the relationship of those proposals to general proposals for the development and other use of land in neighbouring areas, which may be expected to affect that area.

The structure plan is a policy document, and it may not give an individual owner much information about the proposals for his specific piece of land. Such information is more likely to be obtained from a local plan, which may take different forms such as town plans, village plans and action area plans. These plans will establish a planning policy with which individual landowners must comply.

Local planning authorities control the development of land by requiring the developer to obtain planning permission. Development is defined in the Town and Country Planning Act 1971 as 'the carrying out of building, engineering, mining or other operations in, on, over or under land and the making of any material change in the use of any buildings or other land'. To establish whether or not a change of use is material, reference should be made to the Town and Country Planning (Use Classes) Order 1972. For example, changing the use of a cinema to a theatre is not a material change of use, but changing the use of a turf accountant's office to a confectionery shop would be a material change of use.

A prospective developer must make application for planning permission on the appropriate forms to the local planning authority, who has the power to grant unconditionally, grant subject to conditions or refuse planning permission. Where planning permission is granted, it is usually a requirement that the development must be carried out within five years of the permission.

Permission must also be obtained for the provision of new accesses onto highways and display of most advertisements.

The Local Government Planning and Land Act 1980 introduced amendments to planning law to simplify procedure.

Buildings of special architectural or historic interest are protected by the Town and Country Planning Act 1971 and subsequent Regulations. Such buildings may be 'listed' by the Secretary of State; copies of these lists being kept by the Secretary of State, the appropriate local planning authorities and other local authorities.

If a local planning authority is of the opinion that an unlisted building of special architectural or historic interest is in danger of demolition or alteration which would adversely affect its character, it may apply to the Secretary of State to list the building. In the meantime, a building preservation notice would be served on the owner and occupier. Permission must be obtained to demolish, extend or alter listed buildings. Persons carrying out unauthorised works will be liable to imprisonment and/or a fine.

Under the Town and Country Planning Act 1971 and the Town and Country Planning (Amendment) Act 1972, areas of special architectural or historic interest may be designated as 'conservation areas'. Buildings within these areas (even if unlisted) will be subject to local planning authority control.

A local planning authority may also make tree preservation orders as directed by the Town and Country Planning (Tree Preservation Order) Regulations 1969. These may apply to individual trees, groups of trees or woodland areas. Such trees may not be felled, lopped or topped without permission. Local authority powers in relation to conservation areas and the protection of trees have been extended by the Town and Country Amenities Act 1974.

Building and Other Controls

Local authorities have control over the construction of buildings by powers derived from the Building Regulations 1972 and subsequent amendments, and London Constructional Bylaws in the London area. Approval must be obtained before construction of buildings can take

place. Application forms and plans must be submitted to the local
authority. The regulations prescribe the standards of construction and
materials to be used. Officers of the local authority have power to inspect building works as they proceed, at specified stages, and to enforce
the provisions of the Regulations.

Local authorities must implement the provisions of the Offices,
Shops and Railway Premises Act 1963 which are concerned with clean-
liness, overcrowding, temperature, ventilation and lighting of offices,
shops and railway premises; also for the provision of suitable and sufficient sanitary conveniences and washing facilities, the provision of
drinking water, the safety of the premises and machinery, first-aid
facilities and for provision of means of escape in case of fire. This
legislation may require an owner of one of these classes of buildings to
undertake considerable expenditure to put the property in order.

In the case of factories, similar provisions are contained in the
Factories Act 1961; the enforcing authority being the local authority,
or, if the building has mechanical power, the factory inspector.

The Fire Precautions Act 1971 requires that certain premises designated by the Secretary of State for Home Affairs shall have a certificate
issued by the fire authority, which states that the means of escape and
provision for fire fighting and warning of fire are adequate. These
premises include hotels, boarding houses, places of entertainment,
institutions providing treatment or care and those used for purposes of
teaching, training or research.

With regard to housing, local authorities have the power to implement the provisions of the Housing Acts 1957-80. Local authorities
have the right to order owners of insanitary houses to repair them at
reasonable expense or demolish them. They may also declare areas to
be *clearance* areas, where houses (singly or in groups) need to be demolished and the sites redeveloped. *General improvement areas* may be
established under the Housing Act 1969, and in these cases the local
authority may require a landlord to provide standard amenities (bath,
wash basin, water closet, sink and hot and cold water supply) in his
properties. The landlord receives financial assistance through local
authority payment of improvement grants.

The Defective Premises Act 1972 places a duty of care on all persons
concerned with the provision of new dwellings, including conversion and
enlargement of existing buildings. The work is to be done in a workman-
like or professional manner with proper materials so that the dwelling is
fit for habitation. It does not apply to Scotland or Northern Ireland,

nor in those cases where the Secretary of State has approved a scheme which gives equal or better protection to the purchaser, such as the National House-building Council scheme.

The Caravan Sites and Control of Development Act 1960 provides that, subject to certain exemptions specified in the First Schedule of the Act, no occupier of land may allow any part of his land to be used as a caravan site for residential or holiday purposes unless he obtains a site licence. Local authorities have a duty under the Caravan Sites Act 1968 to provide sites for gipsies, and are also given powers to control unauthorised gipsy encampments when there is adequate provision of authorised sites.

CHARACTERISTICS OF LAND AND PROPERTY

The investor in land and property, as with any other source of investment, requires an annual return on his capital; this is obtained by purchasing an interest in real property and obtaining an annual return in the form of rent.

A purchaser of an interest in real property may buy for personal occupation, and he may be in competition with an investor. In his choice of property, a purchaser for personal occupation will pay special attention to the available social and commercial facilities. In the case of housing, these will include proximity to schools, shops, entertainment and employment. The investor will be concerned with yield and will compare with the ideal investment.

A prospective occupier of real property may have the choice between purchasing the freehold interest or leasing. He should consider the advantages, such as security, which purchasing would normally give him. The capital to purchase the premises may be obtained by mortgage borrowing. The occupier should compare the interest repayments on his mortgage with the rent that he would be expected to pay. He will only be prepared to pay more in interest repayments than rent, if the advantages of being a freeholder compared with a lessee make it worthwhile.

There are certain characteristics relating to real property that will affect the security of both capital and income.

External Influences

Land and buildings vary in their condition with consequent effect on value. Variations may arise from natural consequences, such as the nature of the soil and adverse weather conditions, creating such problems as flooding, subsidence and damage due to lightning. Damage may also occur to land and buildings due to human activities such as vandalism, accidental damage, fire and hostilities.

Insurance cover can provide a safeguard against financial loss arising from physical risks, and this may be the responsibility of the landlord or the tenant, according to the terms of the lease. The landlord often insures the premises and recovers the premium from the tenant; the occupant may insure the contents of the premises.

Deterioration of the Structure

The physical life of a building is often difficult to estimate. Building techniques and materials are constantly changing, and it is likely that buildings in the future will not be planned to last as long as they have in the past. However, in order to ensure a reasonable standard for occupation, it will be necessary for sums of money to be expended on repairs and decoration throughout the life of the building.

Standards are constantly changing, so to ensure a reasonable level of rent the property has to be improved and renovated. For example, the occupiers of multi-storey office buildings may expect the latest types of central heating, air conditioning and lift systems. The occupiers of houses may in the future expect central heating to be a standard item.

If the investor is responsible for maintenance of property under the terms of a lease, he may provide for these costs by setting aside an annual sum out of the rent he receives.

The age of a building will also be reflected in the yield that an investor will expect; thus an old building, likely to be demolished in the foreseeable future, will show a higher yield than one with a reasonable life, although the site might have development potential value in excess of the value of the obsolescent building.

Changes in Taste and Demand

The rental value of a building may be reduced because the purpose of the building no longer satisfies a demand. An investor must attempt to anticipate whether or not a building will continue to be functional in its present form, and this will affect the yield he may expect from the investment.

Examples of changes in the use of buildings in recent years are the decline of the local cinema in favour of the bingo hall, the need for public houses to provide more comfortable accommodation and entertainment, in shopping the trends towards the larger self-service unit and the increased popularity of launderettes.

Effect of Adjacent Activities

The value of property may be affected by both existing and proposed developments within the area. A prospective investor should inspect the development plans operative in his area and consult with the local planning authority so as to be aware of any developments that may affect the value of the particular property.

Examples. (i) The provision of motorways or trunk roads, airports and new railway stations will affect the value of all types of property units in that area.

(ii) The building of an industrial estate may be detrimental to neighbouring residential property.

(iii) The provision of a new shopping unit may alter the values of other shops in the vicinity.

(iv) The building of a new further educational establishment may affect property values in the area, because demand will be created for

rented residential accommodation. There may also be an influx of
vehicles into the area.

(v) The building of crematoria, sewage-treatment works and
electricity substations may all reduce the value of surrounding property.

Economic Activities

The demand for land is affected by economic activities and national,
regional and local policies. For example, the New Towns Act 1946
created development corporations to acquire, develop and manage land
for the provision of new towns. These bodies also have the responsibility
for selling or leasing the completed properties. This, obviously, has a
far-reaching effect upon the owners and occupiers of land and buildings
in these locations.

Policies of expanding old towns, improving and altering communications and decentralising offices and industries to less buoyant areas
will affect the land values in the areas concerned.

There may be some areas that are particularly dependent for their
livelihood on a specific economic activity such as coal-mining. If that
activity becomes uneconomic and ceases, then it will have serious effects
upon all types of property in that area. In this situation public authorities, both central and local, will encourage other industries to establish
themselves in the area to maintain a balanced economy.

Changes in Legislation

An investor may not easily anticipate changes in legislation that will
affect property values. Land and property are constantly affected by new
legislation, which may later be repealed when there is a change of
government.

Inflation

Inflationary trends will be a problem with any type of investment. In
the case of fixed-interest securities, the reduction in the real value may
have substantially exceeded the aggregate interest earned over the same
period. The problem will be apparent in the case of property, where the
investor's return (the rent) is a fixed amount to be received over a long

period of time. In this situation, the yield must be high enough to allow for both the depreciation in purchasing power of the fixed amount of rent and a fair return on capital.

To protect himself against the effects of inflation a landlord should make provision for regular reviews of rent when granting a lease. In the past, many ground leases were created with a fixed rent and these were considered to be secure investments. Nowadays these would probably be granted subject to three-year reviews, and this would also be a realistic review period for commercial and residential letting.

The rent to be paid at the review periods may be established in various ways as described below.

(i) The rent may be predetermined at the commencement of the lease. In this case, the landlord must attempt to anticipate the future pattern of inflation as a percentage increase per annum and adjust the current rental value accordingly. This requires expert knowledge of economic trends, and often a landlord will find that he has under-estimated the inflationary increase.

(ii) A better alternative may be to state in the lease when rent is to be reviewed and agreed between the parties. A provision could be included that if the parties fail to agree, the matter will be referred to a qualified valuer. The lease may state that the rent should be reviewed to market value with a stipulation that the rent would not be lower than the existing rent under the lease.

(iii) In commercial property, the rent to be reviewed may be expressed as an agreed percentage on the annual turnover of the business.

(iv) In some cases, the rent may be reviewed by someone other than the parties to the lease. For example, in the case of residential properties protected by the Rent Acts 1965, 1968, 1974 and 1977, a Rent Officer may be requested by landlord, tenant or both to review the rent every two years.

(v) Where new buildings are constructed for investment purposes, the rental values will be influenced by the increase in building costs. An investor will obviously expect a fair return upon his capital cost in the form of rent. If rents do not keep in step with building costs, then the rate of construction of investment properties is likely to slow down. This would create a greater demand by tenants for existing premises and the rents of these would increase accordingly.

Relationship to Other Investment Sources

Land as an investment is in competition with other sources of investment. If yields generally are in an upward direction, then property investments must follow the same pattern, otherwise money will be withdrawn from property and invested elsewhere. Because of the size and nature of the investment, property is usually a long-term investment, which will not be too severely affected by day-to-day market activities unless these persist. However, the availability of credit and borrowing facilities will affect demand for property purchase.

Costs of Transactions

Negotiations involving purchases and sales of land usually take considerable time to complete and involve heavy legal costs compared with other sources of investment.

DETERMINATION OF RENTAL VALUE

The rental value of a commercial property is the amount that a prospective tenant can afford to pay for its occupation. The tenant occupies the property for the purpose of making profit, so that the value of occupation to him will be dependent on what he can earn there. There may be instances where a property has a special value for a particular tenant; for example, the property is adjacent to premises which he already occupies and/or owns.

In the case of residential property, occupation is a need and does not usually serve a profit-making function. In many cases, the rent will be established by statutory rent control, which will determine the maximum amount of rent that may be charged at a particular time.

If rent is dependent on profit, it will be affected by the economic state of the country and many of the characteristics of land and property as previously considered. The rack rental value of property may be calculated at a particular time in several ways.

(i) By reference to the rent currently being paid. This may be a reasonable guide but it could be less than the rack rental value. It may have been fixed at a date in the past, and rental values have since increased due to inflationary trends.

The rent paid may, at the commencement of the lease, be less than the full rental value at that time. This may occur because there is a special relationship between the landlord and tenant such as father and son or the lessor is a parent company of the lessee. Another reason may be that the tenant agrees to pay a capital sum, termed a premium, for the benefit of paying less rent than the rack rental value.

(ii) By comparison with similar property. If properties are owner-occupied, vacant or held on long-established leases, then, to determine their current rental values, it may be necessary to compare them with the general levels of similar properties in the same district. The practical difficulty of this method is that no two properties are exactly the same, so that the value of the comparable property may have to be adjusted to take into account differences in age, location, condition and other matters.

The units of comparison will vary according to the type of land and property; for example, agricultural and building land may be compared per hectare (or acre) and residential, industrial and commercial property per square metre (or square foot) of floor area.

(iii) By considering rent as a proportion of turnover or profit. This method of calculating rack rental value is based on the requirements of the tenant. A prospective tenant of a commercial property will calculate his likely turnover, costs, an allowance for interest on capital employed in the business, salary and rates. The balance will represent profit and he will then determine the proportion of this to be allocated to rent. Hence prospective tenants may differ in the way that they calculate the rent that they are prepared to pay with resultant variations in the figures obtained.

Example. Shop premises are available for letting. *A*, who occupies other premises, wishes to expand his business and estimates that he could earn a profit of £3000 per annum in the shop to be leased. He is prepared to pay 30 per cent of his profit in rent, that is, 30 per cent of £3000 which is £900 per annum.

B, entering into business for the first time, estimates that he could earn a profit of £2000 per annum in this shop. Because he is anxious to commence his own business, he is prepared to pay 50 per cent of his profit in rent, that is, 50 per cent of £2000 which is £1000 per annum.

The landlord would negotiate with *B*, but may not readily accept £1000 per annum, because this would not provide the yield he anticipates from his investment. He has recently purchased the freehold interest in the shop for £15 000. He expects a 7 per cent return, which is £1050 per annum.

The rent eventually paid would be dependent upon the level of demand for the occupancy of the shop.

(iv) By relating the rent to cost. Where land has buildings erected upon it, the rent will consist of two elements. There will be an annual return for the use of the land itself, which will be dependent upon supply and demand. There will also be an annual repayment for the cost of the building, which should be an appropriate yield on the capital outlay.

Example. A has recently purchased a building plot for £10 000. He has built a house on the land, which has cost £30 000. Calculate the rack rental value per annum.

The rack rental value comprises (i) Return on the value of the land

A requires 8 per cent on £10 000 =   £800

(ii) Return on capital outlay of building

A requires 10 per cent on £30 000 =   £3000

Rack rental value per annum =   £3800

This method may be criticised because rent is calculated according to the landlord's expectations and not necessarily what those in the market would be prepared to pay.

RENT AND CAPITAL VALUE

Capital or market value may be defined as the amount of money which may be obtained for an interest at a particular time from those individuals who are able and willing to purchase it.

It has already been established that those able and willing to purchase land and property for investment require a return in the form of rent per annum. However, the investor may incur outgoings, which are annual expenses such as management costs and repairs. These must be deducted from the rent to give the amount which constitutes the true return — the net income per annum. Hence

net income per annum = rent received per annum —
outgoings per annum

If an investor expects a return of 8 per cent per annum from a prospective purchase of property and the net income per annum is £1000, then he will be prepared to purchase at a capital sum of which £1000 is 8 per cent, that is

$$£1000 \times \frac{100}{8} = £12\,500$$

Hence

$$\text{net income per annum} \times \frac{100}{\text{rate of interest}} = \text{capital value}$$

This is termed capitalising the net income and the multiplier is termed years' purchase (YP), so that

$$\text{net income per annum} \times \text{years' purchase} = \text{capital value}$$

OUTGOINGS

The responsibility for the payment of outgoings should be a condition contained in the lease or tenancy agreement.

Leases for a long period (21 years and over) are often full repairing and insuring, that is, the tenant will be responsible for all repairs and insurance. In the case of weekly and monthly tenancies, the landlord is usually responsible for the payment of all outgoings.

The calculation of an annual allowance for landlord's outgoings is necessary in order to arrive at net income per annum. The practical difficulty of calculating outgoings is that they will vary from year to year, due to such matters as increases in repair costs and changes in general and water rates. The amount of liability for outgoings that a landlord incurs under the terms of the lease will affect the security of his interest, so influencing his yield and the years' purchase. The outgoings most commonly taken into account are as follows.

Rent Payable to a Superior Landlord

With a leasehold interest, a lessee may relet the premises to a sublessee. He must deduct from the rent he receives any rent which is payable by him to the freeholder or lessor. This may be a ground rent or an occupation rent.

Repairs

Repairs may be the most difficult of outgoings to assess, and consideration must be given to the age and condition of the property and the terms of the lease. If repairs are the responsibility of the landlord, various methods of estimation are available.

(i) By reference to past costs. If records have been kept for repair costs expended on a particular property over a number of years, these may be used as a basis for estimating an annual allowance. For example, assuming records show annual repair costs over the last five years of £230, £190, £250, £265 and £290, then the average cost per annum is £245 (1225/5). If this is used as an annual allowance, it may be misleading if there is a major item of renovation or rebuilding required in the near future. This item will not be reflected in the previous five years' costs. Taking an average of previous costs will not allow for future increases in costs.

(ii) By a planned maintenance programme. An inspection of the property is carried out and a schedule of dilapidation and repair items prepared. An estimate is made of the periods at which items will need to be carried out and their estimated cost. This is then expressed on an annual basis.

Example. Prepare a planned maintenance programme for a well-built, brick, three-bedroomed, detached house. The landlord is responsible for all repairs and external decoration.

Item	Intervals between items being carried out (years)	Capital cost (£)	Annual cost (£)
Repointing brickwork	25	1000	40
Extensive roof repairs	10	500	50
External decoration	5	500	100
Electrical rewiring	15	200	14
Overhaul of hot-water and central-heating systems	10	200	20
Fencing	10	200	20
Resurfacing of drive	10	300	30
Annual contingency allowance (burst pipes, blocked drains, etc.)			150
Annual repair allowance			£424

This is an example of good estate management because the property will be regularly and efficiently maintained. Landlords will, however, arrive at different amounts according to the frequencies that they use and the estimated costs of the various types of work. The method does not take account of discounting future costs to the present time. (Refer to the present value of £1 – chapter 5.)

(iii) By expressing repairs as a percentage of rack rental value. The two methods previously described of ascertaining a repair allowance are dependent upon having a detailed knowledge of the property. If this is not available, the annual allowance may be expressed as a percentage of net rack rental value. This will vary according to the type of property, but the following figures provide a general guide for use in later calculations.

	External repairs (per cent)	Internal repairs (per cent)
Offices, factories and warehouses	10	5
Shops	5	5
Residential property	30 to 40	10 to 20

In the case of residential property, repairs are a very variable item; indeed local authorities and statutory undertakings may expend most of the rent received from residential property on repairs.

(iv) By the landlord determining what he can afford. A landlord may decide, when he invests in land and property, the maximum amount per annum he can expend on repairs. This is not a good method, because, if a landlord has a pre-fixed allowance, this may not always be sufficient. The Defective Premises Act 1972 states that, where premises are let under a tenancy which puts on the landlord an obligation to the tenant for the maintenance or repair of the premises, the landlord owes to all persons who might reasonably expect to be affected by defects in the state of the premises, a duty to take such care as is reasonable in all the circumstances to see that they are reasonably safe from personal injury or from damage to their property caused by a relevant defect. This duty is owed by the landlord if he knows of the relevant defect either by being notified by the tenant or if he ought in all the circumstances to have known. It is of extreme importance that a landlord inspects his premises regularly and keeps them well maintained.

Insurances

The lease will establish who is responsible for the obtaining of insurance cover in the first instance and who is responsible for the maintaining of adequate cover thereafter. In relation to injuries to third parties, the landlord should have a Property Owner's Liability Policy. He should ensure that this covers his liabilities under the Defective Premises Act 1972.

A lease may be specific setting out the exact risks to be dealt with such as fire, flood and damage due to vandalism. In assessing an annual premium, this will be wholly dependent on the sum insured. The sum insured, based on reinstatement cost, must be assessed competently, taking into account the standard of construction of the actual building. The reinstatement cost should be prepared as a cost estimate by a quantity surveyor. The sum insured should be reviewed at regular intervals to take account of increased building costs. The landlord should also ensure that his policy has adequate provision for loss of rent during a rebuilding period. Special insurance is available for such items as lifts and boilers. The deduction from rent for insurance will be the annual premium paid by the landlord. If this is not known, a percentage of net rack rental value may be taken, a reasonable allowance being 2½ to 5 per cent.

Management

A landlord will need to inspect his property and ensure that his tenant is complying with the obligations contained in the lease. He will also have to collect the rent due to him.

In the case of full repairing and insuring leases, the cost of management may be regarded as a factor affecting security and be reflected in the yield. In weekly and monthly tenancies, however, management may be a costly item because rent is probably collected fortnightly. The amounts may be modest but the time and trouble taken is comparatively extravagant. In these cases, 10 per cent of the net rack rental value may be deducted as an annual outgoing. In properties where services such as porters and lifts are provided, 5 per cent of net rack rental value may be deducted. If management is undertaken by professional experts appointed by the landlord, their scale of fees may give an indication of the amount to be allowed for management.

Landlord's Services

Where a building is let in multiple occupation, it may be convenient
for the landlord to provide certain services himself. This is common
practice in flats and offices, where the landlord may repair and redec-
orate common parts, provide central heating, lighting to common parts,
carpeting, lifts and porters. The landlord may recover his costs by
including an amount in the rent. In this case services should be deducted
from rent as an outgoing, in order to arrive at net income. Alternatively
the landlord may serve an account for services probably at half-yearly
intervals.

The landlord must decide whether the cost of services is to be borne
equally by his tenants or apportioned according to the respective floor
areas occupied by each tenant or by some other method. It is essential
that the landlord attempts to take account of rising costs in the arrangements he makes with his tenants.

Bad Debts and Voids

A landlord may anticipate that there is a risk because his tenant may
default with his rent. There may also be instances where the type of
property attracts tenants who are likely to occupy the premises for
short periods and then terminate their tenancy. The property may not
be relet immediately, so that there may be *voids* in the receipt of rent.
It is not usual to deduct an allowance for bad debts or voids as an outgoing. These are factors that seriously affect security of income and
should be reflected in the yield.

Tithe Redemption Annuity

This originates from the period when tithe was paid by the occupant of
land to the Church. It was usually devoted to the repair of churches, the
upkeep of the clergy and relief of the poor, and was 10 per cent of the
produce of the land, later to be 10 per cent of income (tithe rent-
charge). This was substituted in 1936 by tithe redemption annuity, an
annual charge on the owner of land collected by the Inland Revenue.
This annuity is to be paid over 60 years terminating in 1996. Outstanding annuities may be redeemed voluntarily, but where land is sold or
divided into building plots it must be compulsorily redeemed. The
redemption price is obtained by multiplying the annual charge by a
tithe redemption multiplier, which is based on a rate of interest fixed
by the Treasury.

Rent Charges

A rent charge occurs when an owner of an interest in land sells that
interest at a value less than full market value. In lieu of the reduction
in purchase price, he imposes upon the purchaser an annual charge. This
may be perpetual or for a fixed period of time. This charge will be enforceable upon subsequent owners of that land. For example, a freeholder sells land worth a capital value of £10 000 for the sum of £9000
subject to a rent charge in perpetuity. If he requires the rent charge to
give a 10 per cent return on the capital he has forfeited, then it would
be £100 per annum, which is 10 per cent of £1000.

General and Water and Sewerage Rates

General and water and sewerage rates are usually an occupier's payment;
in certain cases a landlord may pay them to the local authority and
then recoup them from the tenant. If a rent includes rates it is termed an
'inclusive' rent and rates must be deducted as an outgoing. If the
occupant pays his own rates direct to the local authority, the rent is
termed an 'exclusive' rent.

The Valuation Officer of the Board of Inland Revenue has the
authority to prepare a valuation list for those properties which are
subjected to rating. Each rateable hereditament has a *rateable value*
which is assessed taking into account age, size, condition, location and
facilities of the property. The local authority prepares an annual state-
ment of expenses, which sets out how its expenditure will be allocated
in the forthcoming year, and the rate poundage which will provide this
expenditure.

Assuming that a three-bedroomed house has a rateable value of £250
and a general rent in £ of £1.50, then the annual general rates would be
£250 x 1.50 = £375. Water and sewerage rates may be collected by the
local authority acting as agents for the appropriate water authority, and
may be expressed as a rate per £ of rateable value. Considering the
previous example, if the water and sewerage rate is 40p per £ of rateable
value, then the annual water and sewerage rates would be £250 x 0.4
= £100.

CHARACTERISTICS OF DIFFERENT TYPES OF,
AND INTERESTS IN, PROPERTY

Ground Rents

Where ground is let by a freeholder to a lessee (or by a lessee to a sub-lessee) for building operations, it is usually let at a ground rent, which is for the use of the land. Where buildings have been erected upon the land the ground rent is secured because the rent received by the landlord is a small proportion of the full rack rental value of the land and buildings. For example, if a ground rent is £10 per annum and the net rack rental value per annum of the land and buildings is £500, then the ground rent is 50 times secured.

In the past, ground leases have been let for periods varying from 99 to 999 years at a ground rent fixed for the entire period. This situation nowadays is unattractive in terms of investment because the rent being fixed does not provide a hedge against inflation, and an investor will probably expect a return in excess of 10 per cent.

With recent ground leases landlords have often required periodic rent reviews; the amount of rent to be paid at each review probably being a percentage of the rack rental value of the land and buildings. The rent to be paid during the building period may be a *peppercorn rent*, a minimal amount. The yield expected by an investor will depend upon the length of the lease, the periods for rent reviews and the type of building.

Agricultural Land

Agricultural land is regarded as a secure type of investment and in recent years has proved to be attractive to institutional investors. Rental values will be dependent on

(i) The general situation of the land, which affects the market for produce and the availability of labour.

(ii) The topography of the land and climate of the district.

(iii) The size of the holding. Generally, smaller farms will yield a higher rent per hectare (acre) than a larger one.

(iv) Natural features such as type and condition of the soil, level of the water table and type and condition of hedges.

(v) The condition of fences and approach roads and the efficiency of land drainage.

(vi) Availability of services such as water supply to both farm buildings and troughs, main drainage and electricity.

(vii) The provision and condition of dwellings and farm buildings. Buildings must be of suitable construction for the housing of livestock and machinery and the storage of crops and fertilisers. Dwellings for employees are a desirable requirement since they may be the means of attracting labour; they should, however, at least have the standard amenities.

The rents of agricultural holdings may be reviewed every three years, and tenants are usually responsible for repairs and maintenance of land and buildings. The landlord may retain responsibility for the structural parts of the farmhouse; if the lease does not mention repair responsibilities then the provisions of the Agriculture (Maintenance, Repair and Insurance of Fixed Equipment) Regulations 1973 will apply.

Successive governments have attempted to ensure that the agricultural industry is encouraged by subsidies and grants to increase production and carry out improvements. The industry is being reorganised as part of the agricultural policy of the European Economic Community. The production methods of the industry have been streamlined during recent years with improved machinery and the grouping of small holdings into larger businesses operated by companies.

Residential Properties

Flats. The majority of flats are built for sale and not for renting. When flats are built for renting, they are mainly provided by local authorities and often incorporated in a development with other types of property.

The private investor may find that the building of flats is prohibitive, because of the high and increasing cost of construction. Some flats, however, are provided by Housing Associations, which are voluntary, independent and non-profit-making bodies. Where flats are available for rent, they are usually considered to be a good investment. The rental value will be dependent upon the condition and locality of the premises, the availability of services, lifts and boilers, and the provision of services such as porterage and cleaning.

Dwelling houses. Over 50 per cent of the housing stock in the United Kingdom is owner-occupied. New houses built in the private sector are seldom made available for renting because there is little incentive for private developers to build and lease. Hence local authorities are given wide powers to acquire land and provide schemes of rented accommodation.

Dwelling houses that are let are subjected to considerable legislation relating to security of tenure and rent control. In many instances, landlords are restricted as to the amount of rent they can charge for their property. The carrying out of repairs and the provision of insurance cover is often the responsibility of the landlord, and in many cases this may prove to be a costly outgoing.

The yield expected by an investor will obviously vary considerably, being dependent upon the age, locality and condition of the property, the age and type of tenant and whether or not the property is subject to rent control.

Shops

The pattern of shopping has varied considerably over the last twenty years, and the many categories of shops can be classified as

Hypermarkets. These are large-scale developments trading as single concerns on a self-service basis with good communications and car parking for at least 1000 cars. They usually provide a considerable range of competitively priced products because of the substantial turnover.

Regional shopping centres. These are located on out-of-town sites and rely on attracting the car-borne shopper. They incorporate branches of national department stores and provide a wider range of shops and a greater selection of luxury goods than hypermarkets. They may also provide community facilities.

Central area shops. Shops on prime sites in towns and cities and those incorporated in new urban developments are very much in demand by prospective tenants and this is reflected in their rental value. Because of the location secure tenants, such as established multiple-store companies, will often compete for the occupation of these sites. The amount of trading may be influenced considerably by the amount of car parking facilities for shoppers.

Suburban shops. Despite the existence of large urban shopping centres, there will still be a demand by local residents for shops on the outskirts of towns and cities. These shops will provide services to their customers that are required at less than weekly intervals, such as provision of food, newspapers and postal services.

Local shops. This type of shop, probably occupied by a sole trader, is usually located within a residential area and provides a convenience service. The success of local shops has in the past largely stemmed from the varied range of goods they provide, the extensive hours of opening and personal service.

Location is obviously important in determining the rental value of shop premises, but there are also other factors

(i) The area of frontage and its layout for the display of goods. A prospective tenant will need to decide whether or not he should renew the shop front.

(ii) The condition of the property and its sanitary arrangements. The property must comply with the requirements of the Offices, Shops and Railway Premises Act 1963.

(iii) The layout of the interior and standard of lighting.

(iv) Access at the rear for delivery. This is an advantage, where there are parking restrictions at the front of the property.

(v) Any upper floors within the premises. These may be used as part of the shop or they could be let separately as offices or residential accommodation.

From an investment viewpoint, the type of business of an existing tenant may affect the yield. Certain businesses such as those dealing in essential foodstuffs and other necessities are generally secure. There may be more risks for businesses dealing in luxury items, such as electrical goods.

Offices

The types of premises used as offices may be converted dwelling-houses, part of a mixed development or purpose-built office accommodation. In areas where restrictions on the provision of new accommodation are imposed, demand will increase for existing office space and rentals will increase. Evidence of this can be found in the central area of London, where rents are probably five or six times higher than for similar premises in provincial cities.

The following factors are relevant when assessing rental value and considering the accommodation as an investment medium.

(i) The premises must comply with the Offices, Shops and Railway Premises Act 1963.

(ii) The location of the office may be an influence on the obtaining of suitable staff. For example women may be more attracted to working in a central area than out-of-town.

(iii) If the building is let to a number of tenants, it may command more rent than if let to a single tenant. However, the extent of management by the landlord may increase, where there are more tenants in the building. Generally, landlords prefer to let to a single tenant of good standing.

(iv) The terms of leases may differ considerably. If offices in a building are let to several tenants, the landlord may retain responsibility for repair of the structure and common parts of the building.

(v) The landlord may provide certain services such as lighting, heating, carpeting, porterage and lifts. The cost may be recovered as part of the rent or as a separate service charge collected each six months or annually.

(vi) In high-rise buildings rents may vary from one floor to another. For example, the lower floors may be considered to have more prestige value than upper floors, although this will depend upon the quality of the building and efficiency of lift services.

There is every indication that demand for office accommodation will continue, particularly for small units in central areas.

Industrial Premises

The demand for factories and warehouses is dependent upon the economic state of industry and the capacity of firms to expand, and the provision of new industrial accommodation.

Recently, there has been an upsurge of demand for rented industrial accommodation particularly for purpose-built units. There is, however, a large amount of obsolete premises which need to be demolished and rebuilt.

Central government has attempted to create new industrial space by designating enterprise zones, which are given tax and rate relief. Capital expenditure on the development of certain industrial buildings may qualify for Industrial Building Allowances.

Location in relation to transport systems, availability of labour and markets is an important factor, but the following should also be considered.

(i) The construction, condition and facilities of the buildings. The premises must comply with the requirements of Factories Acts with regard to such items as means of escape in case of fire, heating, ventilation, natural light and sanitary accommodation.

(ii) The general layout of the buildings. The buildings should have good facilities for delivery and despatch of goods, storage and handling. The height of the buildings may be important for certain manufacturing processes. It will be an advantage if the buildings can be readily adapted for other uses.

(iii) The provision of facilities for employees such as car parking, canteens and social areas, (for example, bars and games rooms).

There has been a tendency in the past for the investor not to favour industrial premises as his first choice of investment. However, at present, there seems to be more confidence in investment within this type of property.

Other Types of Property

The valuation of more specialised types of property such as cinemas, theatres and hotels and interests connected with minerals and sporting rights are considered to be beyond the scope of this book.

PATTERNS OF YIELDS

Table 4.1 indicates suggested yields which investors may expect from different types of property. It must be emphasised that this table gives a general guide only, and yields will frequently be fluctuating depending upon the investment market.

Table 4.1   Suggested Yields for Property Investments (yields for freehold interests let on a rack rental basis)

Description of property	Yield (per cent)	Remarks
Tenement-type housing	14 to 20	Property usually in poor condition with owner responsible for repairs—statutory rent control—tenants may be poor payers—no market for sale
Dwelling houses—good condition	8 to 10	Large numbers of such properties may be subjected to statutory rent control
Dwelling houses—poor condition	10 to 12	As above, but landlord's repair responsibility may be extensive—no market for sale with tenant in occupation
Flats	5 to 8	Good investment particularly in well-established urban areas
Factories and warehouses	6 to 14	Dependent on whether premises have been designed for one particular trade or are adaptable; also location, proximity to transport systems, availability of labour
Offices	4 to 9	Varies according to design and location, amount of management cost to be borne by the owner
Shops	4 to 9	Depends on position, type of unit and type of tenant (e.g. multiple, small trader)
Agricultural land	3 to 6	Government assistance—repairs usually undertaken by tenant—3-year rent reviews
Freehold ground rents (secured)	5 to 7 or 10 to 20	Secure investment if a short unexpired term and periodic increases in rent Long unexpired term—fixed income

5 CONSTRUCTION AND ANALYSIS OF VALUATION TABLES

In valuation and land use practice it is necessary to undertake calculations that are usually based upon compound interest principles. Valuation tables have been constructed to eliminate much of the time-consuming aspect of calculation work.

The tables to be studied in this chapter will be considered under three broad headings

(i) Single Rate tables
(ii) Dual Rate tables
(iii) Mortgage Instalment table

The tables are based upon the £1 unit, unless specifically stated otherwise. The following abbreviations will be used

i = rate of interest per annum expressed as a decimal
n = term of years (or number of periods of interest accumulation)
s = annual sinking fund to be invested to accumulate to £1 after a given number of years at a certain rate of compound interest.

The calculations in this chapter have been worked out using logarithms. The valuation tables are compiled with the use of a computer, so that there may be slight differences between the figures calculated from formulae and the valuation table figures.

SINGLE RATE TABLES

Amount of £1 (A)

This is the amount to which £1 invested now will accumulate at i compound interest in n years. It is assumed that interest is added annually at the end of each year. This is the compound interest table, and the formula was proved in chapter 2.

$$A = (1 + i)^n$$

Example. To what amount will £1 invested at 6 per cent compound interest accumulate in 4 years?

$$A = (1 + i)^n$$
$$= (1 + 0.06)^4$$
$$= 1.06^4$$
$$= £1.263$$

The table assumes that the compound interest will be added annually; there will be many instances where interest is payable at intervals less than this, such as half-yearly, quarterly and monthly. The formula may be adjusted to take account of this, by observing the following rules.

(i) divide *i* by the number of interest accumulations in the year

(ii) multiply *n* by the number of interest accumulations in the year

If the interest is accumulating half-yearly, the formula becomes

$$A = (1 + \frac{i}{2})^{2n}$$

and quarterly

$$A = (1 + \frac{i}{4})^{4n}$$

Referring to the previous example, to what amount will £1 invested at 6 per cent accumulate in 4 years

(i) if interest is payable half-yearly

(ii) if interest is payable quarterly?

(i)
$$A = \left(1 + \frac{i}{2}\right)^{2n}$$
$$= 1.03^8$$
$$= £1.266$$

(Valuation tables give a figure of 1.2668.)

(ii)
$$A = (1 + \frac{i}{4})^{4n}$$
$$= 1.015^{16}$$
$$= £1.266$$

(Valuation tables give a figure of 1.2690.)

Example. To what amount will £100 invested at 15 per cent rate of interest accumulate in 8 years, if interest is payable monthly?

$$A = \left(1 + \frac{i}{12}\right)^{12n}$$

$$= \left(1 + \frac{0.15}{12}\right)^{12 \times 8}$$

$$= 1.0125^{96}$$

$$= 3.227$$

(Valuation tables give a figure of 3.2955.) For £100

$$A = 3.227 \times 100$$

$$= £323$$

The Amount of £1 table forms the basis for all subsequent valuation tables.

Present Value of £1 (PV)

This is the amount that must be invested now to accumulate to £1 at i compound interest in n years. The formula for this table may be constructed as follows

(i) Assume £1 is invested at i for 1 year; then at the end of the year the accumulation will be $£(1 + i)$.

(ii) Assume x (an unknown) is invested at i for 1 year, and at the end of the year the accumulation will be £1.

In (i) £1 is the Present Value (PV). In (ii) x is the Present Value (PV).

$$x : 1 = 1 : 1 + i$$

so that

$$x = \frac{1}{1 + i}$$

Thus

$$PV = \frac{1}{(1 + i)^n}$$

This is the reciprocal of the Amount of £1 table.

Example. What amount must be invested now at 8 per cent to accumulate to £1 in 7 years' time?

$$PV = \frac{1}{(1 + i)^n}$$

$$\frac{1}{1.08^7} = \frac{1}{1.713}$$

$$= £0.583$$

The Present Value of £1 table gives the current value of the right to receive £1 at a known future date. This Present Value is termed the *deferred value* of a future sum. The table may also be used to calculate the capital sum to be invested now to provide for a known future liability.

Example. A man has the right to receive £1000 in 12 years' time. What is the present value of this right, assuming that capital could be invested at $7\frac{1}{2}$ per cent compound interest?

$$PV = \frac{1}{(1 + i)^n}$$

$$= \frac{1}{1.075^{12}}$$

$$= \frac{1}{2.381}$$

$$= 0.419$$

For £1 000

$$PV = 0.419 \times £1\,000 = £419$$

Example. The owner of a house anticipates that he will need to renew a roof at an estimated cost of £850 in 6 years' time. Assuming that capital could be invested at $9\frac{1}{4}$ per cent compound interest, what must he invest now to meet his future liability (ignoring inflation)?

$$PV \text{ of } £1 = \frac{1}{(1 + i)^n}$$

$$= \frac{1}{1.0925^6}$$

$$= \frac{1}{1.7} = 0.588$$

For £850

$$PV = 0.588 \times £850$$

$$= £499.8$$

The Amount of £1 per Annum

This is the amount to which £1 invested at the end of each year will accumulate at i compound interest in n years. The formula for this table is compiled as follows.

If interest is not paid until the end of the first year, the first £1 invested will accumulate for $(n - 1)$ years and the second £1 for $(n - 2)$ years; this pattern will continue until the investment of the last £1, which will gain no interest. Hence the amount of £1 per annum $= (1 + i)^{n-1} + (1 + i)^{n-2}$ ... up to and including $(1 + i)^2 + (1 + i) + 1$.

If these terms are reversed for convenience, then the amount of £1 per annum $= 1 + (1 + i) + (1 + i)^2$ ... up to and including $(1 + i)^{n-1}$.

This series of terms is a geometrical progression and it was shown in chapter 3 that the general expression for the sum of such terms is

$$Sn = \frac{a(r^n - 1)}{r - 1}$$

In this series Sn may be substituted by the amount of £1 per annum; a by 1; r by $(1 + i)$ so that

$$\text{Amount of £1 per annum} = \frac{1 (1 + i)^n - 1}{(1 + i) - 1}$$

$$= \frac{(1 + i)^n - 1}{i} \text{ or } \frac{A - 1}{i}$$

(where A = amount of £1.)

Example. £100 is invested at the end of each year in a building society giving $6\frac{1}{2}$ per cent compound interest. To what amount will this accumulate after 20 years?

$$\text{Amount of £1 per annum} = \frac{(1+i)^n - 1}{i}$$

$$= \frac{1.065^{20} - 1}{0.065}$$

$$= \frac{3.516 - 1}{0.065} = \frac{2.516}{0.065}$$

$$= 38.7$$

(Valuation tables give a figure of 38.8253.) For £100, accumulation will be

$$38.7 \times £100 = £3870$$

This table is therefore derived from the addition of the amounts of £1 for each £1 invested over the period of n years.

Example. Calculate the Amount of £1 per annum for 3 years at 6 per cent compound interest.

(i) By the addition of the Amounts of £1

$$(1+i)^{n-1} + (1+i)^{n-2} + 1$$

$$= 1.06^2 + 1.06^1 + 1$$

$$= 1.123 + 1.06 + 1$$

$$= 3.183$$

(ii) By using the formula $[(1+i)^n - 1]/i$

$$= \frac{(1.06)^3 - 1}{0.06}$$

$$= \frac{1.191 - 1}{0.06} = \frac{0.191}{0.06}$$

$$= 3.183$$

Annual Sinking Fund (s)

This is the annual sum, s, required to be invested at the end of each year to accumulate to £1 in n years at i compound interest.

Since the Present Value of £1 is the reciprocal of the Amount of £1, so the Annual Sinking Fund is the reciprocal of the Amount of £1 per annum. The formula is

$$s = \frac{i}{(1 + i)^n - 1} \text{ or } \frac{i}{A - 1}$$

The Annual Sinking Fund may be used to calculate the annual amount to be set aside to meet a known future liability or expense.

Example. The owner of a house anticipates that he will need to provide a new staircase in 10 years' time at an estimated cost of £700. If capital can be invested at 8 per cent compound interest, what amount should be invested annually to meet his future liability?

$$s = \frac{i}{(1 + i)^n - 1}$$

$$= \frac{0.08}{1.08^{10} - 1}$$

$$= \frac{0.08}{2.158 - 1} = \frac{0.08}{1.158}$$

$$= 0.069$$

So that the Annual Sinking Fund to provide £700

$$= 0.069 \times £700$$

$$= £48.3$$

The formula assumes that the sinking fund payment would be made at the end of the year. Where payments have to be made at the beginning of each year, the formula would be adjusted to

$$\frac{i}{(1 + i)^{n+1} - 1}$$

Example. Calculate the Annual Sinking Fund to produce £1 in 21 years at 7 per cent assuming the payment will be made (i) at the beginning of each year, and (ii) at the end of each year.

(i)
$$s = \frac{i}{(1+i)^{n+1} - 1}$$

$$= \frac{0.07}{1.07^{22} - 1}$$

$$= \frac{0.07}{4.43 - 1} = \frac{0.07}{3.43}$$

$$= 0.0204$$

(ii)
$$s = \frac{i}{(1+i)^{n} - 1}$$

$$= \frac{0.07}{1.07^{21} - 1}$$

$$= \frac{0.07}{4.14 - 1} = \frac{0.07}{3.14}$$

$$= 0.022$$

Years' Purchase (YP) or Present Value of £1 per Annum

This is the present value of the right to receive £1 at the end of each year for n years at i compound interest. The formula is derived from the addition of the Present Values of £1 for each £1 received. Thus

$$\text{PV of £1 due in 1 year} = \frac{1}{1+i}$$

$$\text{PV of £1 due in 2 years} = \frac{1}{(1+i)^2}$$

$$\text{Years' Purchase for 2 years} = \frac{1}{1+i} + \frac{1}{(1+i)^2}$$

Thus

$$\text{Years' Purchase for } n \text{ years} = \frac{1}{1+i} + \frac{1}{(1+i)^2} + \frac{1}{(1+i)^3} \quad \cdots$$

$$\text{up to and including } \frac{1}{(1+i)^{n-1}} + \frac{1}{(1+i)^n} \tag{5.1}$$

Multiply both sides by $(1+i)$ and call the resultant equation (5.2).

Years' Purchase for n years $\times (1 + i) = \dfrac{1+i}{1+i} + \dfrac{1+i}{(1+i)^2} + \dfrac{1+i}{(1+i)^3} \;\cdots$

up to and including $\dfrac{1+i}{(1+i)^{n-1}} + \dfrac{1+i}{(1+i)^n}$ (5.2)

This can be expressed as

Years' Purchase for n years $\times (1 + i) = 1 + \dfrac{1}{1+i} + \dfrac{1}{(1+i)^2} \;\cdots$

up to and including $\dfrac{1}{(1+i)^{n-2}} + \dfrac{1}{(1+i)^{n-1}}$

Subtract equation 5.1 from equation 5.2 giving the Year's Purchase for n years $\times (1 + i)$ — the Years' Purchase for n years as

$$1 - \dfrac{1}{(1+i)^n}$$

This is Years' Purchase for n years $+ i$ (Years' Purchase for n years) — Years' Purchase for n years which equals

$$1 - \dfrac{1}{(1+i)^n}$$

i (Years' Purchase for n years) $= 1 - \dfrac{1}{(1+i)^n}$

Years' Purchase for n years = $\dfrac{1 - \dfrac{1}{(1+i)^n}}{i}$ or $\dfrac{1 - PV}{i}$
  (YP)

(where PV = Present Value of £1.)

    This table gives the multiplier which can be applied to an income receivable at the end of each year for n years at i compound interest in order to find its present capital value.

Example. A landlord will receive £100 per annum rent from his tenant for the next 20 years. Assuming 8 per cent compound interest, what is the capital value of the income?

YP for 20 years at 8 per cent $= \dfrac{1 - \dfrac{1}{(1+i)^n}}{i}$

$$= \frac{1 - \dfrac{1}{1.08^{20}}}{0.08}$$

$$= \frac{1 - \dfrac{1}{4.66}}{0.08} = \frac{1 - 0.2145}{0.08}$$

$$= \frac{0.7855}{0.08}$$

$$= 9.818$$

So that

capital value of £100 per annum = 9.818 × £100

= £981.8

This may be more conveniently set out as follows

rent received per annum	£100
YP for 20 years at 8 per cent	9.818
Capital value =	£981.8

The use of a single-rate YP table assumes that the income being valued will be followed by another stream of income (see p. 72 on Dual rate tables).

Years' Purchase in Perpetuity (YP)

This is the present value of the right to receive £1 at the end of each year in perpetuity at i compound interest. This differs from the previous table in that the income is received not for a limited period of time but for perpetuity, that is, an endless period of time. If the income at the end of each year is £1, and the investor requires a return (or *net income*) of say 8 per cent (i) then £1 is 8 per cent of the capital value. So that

$$YP = \frac{1}{0.08} = 12.5 \text{ giving the formula}$$

$$YP \text{ in perpetuity} = \frac{1}{i}$$

This YP can be multiplied to any perpetual income receivable at the end of each year at i compound interest.

Example. A is the owner of a freehold interest in a shop yielding a net income of £250 per annum. Assuming 7 per cent compound interest, calculate the capital value of A's interest.

$$\text{Net income per annum} = £250$$

$$\text{YP in perpetuity at 7 per cent} = \frac{1}{i} = \frac{1}{0.07} = \underline{14.286}$$

$$\text{Capital value} = £3571$$

The valuation tables do not contain separate tables for Years' Purchase in perpetuity; the required figures may be found at the bottom of each column in the Years' Purchase or Present Value of £1 per annum table.

Years' Purchase of a Reversion to a Perpetuity

This is the present value of the right to receive £1 at the end of each year in perpetuity at i compound interest, but receivable after the expiration of n years.

It has been established that, if £1 is receivable at the end of each year in perpetuity, then its capital value (YP) = $1/i$. However, this YP would not be paid for a stream of income that was not receivable until n years had expired. The present value of such income would be the amount that could be invested now at i to produce $1/i$ in n years; this is the PV of $1/i$.

The YP of a reversion to a perpetuity is given by

$$\text{PV of £1} \times \frac{1}{i}$$

$$= \frac{1}{(1+i)^n} \times \frac{1}{i}$$

$$= \frac{1}{i(1+i)^n} \text{ or } \frac{1}{iA}$$

Example. What is the capital value of the right to receive £1 per annum in perpetuity commencing in 7 years' time? (Assume 7 per cent compound interest.)

$$YP = \frac{1}{i(1+i)^n}$$

$$= \frac{1}{0.07 \times 1.07^7}$$

$$= \frac{1}{0.07 \times 1.606} = \frac{1}{0.1124}$$

$$= 8.896$$

This would be set out as follows

Net income per annum $\qquad = £1$

YP in perpetuity at 7 per cent $\quad = \dfrac{1}{i}$

$$= \frac{1}{0.07} = 14.286$$

PV of £1 for 7 years at 7 per cent

$$= \frac{1}{(1+i)^n} = \frac{1}{1.07^7} = \underline{0.6227}$$

YP in perpetuity deferred 7 years at 7 per cent = $\underline{8.896}$

Capital value = £8.896

This table will be used for the valuation of reversions in freehold interests.

Example. The owner of freehold property will receive net income of £275 per annum, commencing in 4 years' time. Assuming a return of 8 per cent, value his interest.

Net income per annum $\qquad = £275$

YP in perpetuity deferred 4 years at 8 per cent

$$= \frac{1}{i(1+i)^n}$$

$$= \frac{1}{0.08 \times 1.08^4} = \frac{1}{0.08 \times 1.36}$$

$$= \frac{1}{0.109} = \underline{9.18}$$

Capital value = £2524

Interest at Intervals of Less than One Year

The Single Rate tables analysed in this chapter have been based on the assumption that the interest would accumulate at annual intervals. Interest may accumulate at periods less than the year such as half-yearly, quarterly and monthly; this was considered earlier in this chapter with the Amount of £1. The rule in these situations is

(i) Divide *i* by the number of interest accumulations in the year
(ii) Multiply *n* by the number of interest accumulations in the year

In the same way, other tables may be modified.

Example. Find the capital value of an income of £200 per annum for 12 years at 8 per cent compound interest.

Income per annum   = £200

YP for 12 years at 8 per cent

$$= \frac{1 - \dfrac{1}{(1+i)^n}}{i} \quad = \frac{1 - \dfrac{1}{1.08^{12}}}{0.08}$$

$$= \frac{1 - 0.397}{0.08} \quad = \frac{0.603}{0.08} \quad = \underline{7.54}$$

Capital value = £1508

If the interest were credited half-yearly, there would be 24 separate incomes of £100 each at 4 per cent compound interest for each half-year. The amended calculation would be

Net income per period   = £100

YP for 24 periods at 4 per cent per period

$$= \frac{1 - \dfrac{1}{(1+i)^n}}{i} \quad = \frac{1 - \dfrac{1}{1.04^{24}}}{0.04}$$

$$= \frac{1 - 0.39}{0.04} \quad = \frac{0.61}{0.04} \quad = \underline{15.25}$$

Capital value = £1525

Income to be Received at Intervals of more than One Year

There may be circumstances where income is received not at the end of each year but at greater intervals. The capital value may be calculated by using the formula

capital value = amount of each payment X

$$\left(\frac{\text{YP for the total term}}{\text{YP for period between payments}}\right) \times \begin{array}{l}\text{PV of £1 for period before}\\\text{receipt of first payment}\end{array}$$

Example. What is the capital value of the right to receive 5 payments each of £100, these being received at 5 year intervals? (Assume 8 per cent compound interest.)

Each payment = £100

$$\frac{\text{YP for the total term}}{\text{YP for period between payments}} \times \begin{array}{l}\text{PV of £1 for period before}\\\text{receipt of first payment}\end{array}$$

$$= \frac{\text{YP for 25 years at 8 per cent}}{\text{YP for 5 years at 8 per cent}} \times \text{PV of £1 for 5 years at 8 per cent}$$

$$= \frac{10.67}{3.99} \times 0.681 \qquad = \underline{1.821}$$

Capital value = £182.1

The parts of the formula are calculated as follows.

$$\text{YP for 25 years at 8 per cent} = \frac{1 - \dfrac{1}{1.08^{25}}}{0.08} = \frac{1 - 0.1462}{0.08}$$

$$= 10.67$$

$$\text{YP for 5 years at 8 per cent} = \frac{1 - \dfrac{1}{1.08^{5}}}{0.08} = \frac{1 - 0.681}{0.08}$$

$$= 3.99$$

$$\text{PV of £1 for 5 years at 8 per cent} = \frac{1}{1.08^{5}} = 0.681$$

Without using the formula, the answer could be established as follows

Each payment   = £100

PV of £1 for 5 years at 8 per cent = 0.681

10 years at 8 per cent = 0.463

15 years at 8 per cent = 0.316

20 years at 8 per cent = 0.215

25 years at 8 per cent = 0.146

= 1.821

Capital value   = £182.1

QUESTIONS

Without the use of valuation tables, evaluate the following.

5.1   The Amount of £1 for 15 years at 9 per cent compound interest.

5.2   The Present Value of £1 for 14 years at $7\frac{1}{2}$ per cent compound interest.

5.3   The capital value of the right to receive £150 per annum for 8 years at $8\frac{1}{2}$ per cent compound interest.

5.4   The Annual Sinking fund to produce £250 in 16 years at 6 per cent compound interest.

5.5   The capital value of a freehold interest in property yielding a net income of £225 per annum. The income will commence in 5 years' time. Assume 8 per cent compound interest.

5.6   The present liability to an owner of property, who anticipates he will need to spend £200 in 5 years' time to renew a staircase and a further £500 in 8 years' time to carry out roof repairs. Assume that capital could be invested at 6 per cent compound interest.

DUAL RATE TABLES

Years' Purchase or Present Value of £1 per Annum (YP)

This is the capital value of the right to receive £1 at the end of each year for *n* years at *i* compound interest, but allowing for a sinking fund *s* to recoup the original capital after 'n' years.

Dual Rate tables should be used for calculating the capital value of income that is to be received for a known limited period. This will occur in land and property with leashold interests that will expire on a specified date.

If an interest has income that is receivable for a limited period only, the purchaser could not afford to pay the same amount as for the purchasing of a perpetual stream of income. At the end of the period the income would cease and the original capital (purchase price) would be lost. Dual Rate tables are based on the assumption that the investor would annually set aside a sum out of the income received. This would be invested as a sinking fund to recoup the original capital at the end of the term. The Years' Purchase must reflect the fact that the investor has a lower *spendable income* than in the case of the perpetual income.

Example. What is the capital value of £100 per annum receivable in perpetuity? The owner requires an 8 per cent return.

$$\text{Net income per annum} \qquad = £100$$

YP in perpetuity at 8 per cent

$$= \frac{1}{i} = \frac{1}{0.08} \qquad\qquad = \underline{12.5}$$

$$\text{Capital value} = £1250$$

If the stream of income is receivable for 25 years only, then the capital value could be calculated as follows.

Assume the capital value to be *x*. The sinking fund to recoup *x* at the end of 25 years should be invested at a risk-free net rate of interest such as $2\frac{1}{2}$ per cent. (This is referred to as an *accumulative* rate of interest.) Hence

Net income per annum   = £100

Less s to recoup £1 in 25 years at $2\frac{1}{2}$ per cent

$$= \frac{i}{(1+i)^n - 1} = \frac{0.025}{1.025^{25} - 1} = 0.029$$

s to recoup x in 25 years at $2\frac{1}{2}$ per cent = $\underline{0.029x}$

Spendable income per annum = $100 - 0.029x$

YP in perpetuity at 8 per cent = 12.5

Capital value   = $\underline{1250 - 0.3625x}$

The capital value is x, thus

$$1250 - 0.3625x = x$$

$$1250 = 1.3625x$$

$$x = \frac{1250}{1.3625}$$

Capital value = £917

This capital value could have been calculated by using the Dual Rate YP table, which is constructed as follows.

Assume the net interest on £1 to be i and the annual sinking fund to recoup £1 at the end of the limited term to be s. Then the total income from property worth a capital value of £1 = $i + s$. Assume the capital value of a stream of income to be P. Then the annual income required is $P(i + s)$. But

Capital value = Net income per annum × YP

So that

$$\text{YP} = \frac{P}{P(i + s)}$$

$$\text{YP} = \frac{1}{i + s}$$

In this formula, there are two different rates of interest

(i) i is the rate of interest expected by the investor (known as a *remunerative* rate of interest).

(ii) the rate of interest for s is a low, risk-free rate (an *accumulative* rate of interest).

Referring to the previous example of income of £100 per annum receivable for 25 years only, this can now be calculated using the Dual Rate YP formula.

$$\text{Net income per annum} = £100$$

YP for 25 years at 8 per cent and $2\frac{1}{2}$ per cent

$$= \frac{1}{i+s} = \frac{1}{i + \dfrac{i}{(1+i)^n - 1}}$$

$$= \frac{1}{0.08 + \dfrac{0.025}{1.025^{25} - 1}}$$

$$= \frac{1}{0.08 + 0.029}$$

$$= \frac{1}{0.109} = \underline{9.17}$$

$$\text{Capital value} = £917$$

Example. What is the capital value of an income of £500 per annum receivable for 12 years only? The investor requires an 8 per cent return.

$$\text{Net income per annum} = £500$$

YP for 12 years at 8 per cent and $2\frac{1}{2}$ per cent

$$= \frac{1}{i+s} = \frac{1}{i + \dfrac{i}{(1+i)^n - 1}}$$

$$= \frac{1}{0.08 + \dfrac{0.025}{1.025^{12} - 1}}$$

$$= \frac{1}{0.08 + 0.0726}$$

$$= \frac{1}{0.1526} \qquad = \underline{6.553}$$

$$\text{Capital value} = \text{£3276}$$

This can be checked as follows.

$$\text{Net income per annum} = \text{£500}$$

Less s to recoup £3276 in 12 years at $2\frac{1}{2}$ per cent

$$= 0.0726 \times 3276 \qquad\qquad = \underline{237.83}$$

$$\text{Spendable income per annum} \qquad \text{£262.17}$$

$$\text{YP in perpetuity at 8 per cent} \qquad \underline{12.5}$$

$$\text{Capital value} = \text{£3277}$$

(The £1 discrepancy has occurred because of the 'rounding-off' of figures.)

Referring to an earlier section of this chapter, the Single Rate YP was calculated from the formula

$$\frac{1 - \frac{1}{(1 + i)^n}}{i}$$

It may appear that this does not incorporate a sinking fund element as in the Dual Rate YP. However, Dual Rate tables could be used in a Single Rate situation, but the rate of interest to be used for the sinking fund element would be the same as for i, the remunerative rate of interest.

Example. Calculate the YP (Single Rate) for 10 years at 6 per cent.

Using the Single Rate formula

$$\text{YP} = \frac{1 - \frac{1}{(1 + i)^n}}{i}$$

$$= \frac{1 - \frac{1}{1.06^{10}}}{0.06}$$

$$= \frac{1 - 0.5583}{0.06} = \frac{0.4417}{0.06}$$

$$= 7.36$$

Using the Dual Rate formula

$$\text{YP} = \frac{1}{i+s} = \cfrac{1}{i + \cfrac{i}{(1+i)^n - 1}}$$

$$= \cfrac{1}{0.06 + \cfrac{0.06}{1.06^{10} - 1}}$$

$$= \frac{1}{0.06 + 0.0758} = \frac{1}{0.1358}$$

$$= 7.36$$

The Effect of Tax on the Sinking Fund Element of the Dual Rate YP

No reference has been made in earlier sections of this chapter to the effect of tax on incomes being received. The net income receivable from property (that is, rent) is normally taxable. It is often considered that the tax is on the person and not the property, so that the tax on income is often ignored in the calculation of capital values.

However, in the dual rate calculation, a proportion of income is assumed to be set aside for the provision of a sinking fund. This sinking fund has been allocated in the case of the leasehold interest because the income is for a limited period and is subject to tax. Not only is the sinking fund element (the amount set aside annually) taxed, but also the interest, which accumulates each year. The Dual Rate YP formula must be adjusted to take account of this tax liability.

The accumulative rate of interest must be incorporated in the formula as a net rate of interest adjusted for tax. A gross rate of interest may be reduced to a net figure by multiplying by the net adjustment factor, T_N, where

$$T_N = 1 - x$$

where

$$x = \frac{\text{Rate of tax (new pence)}}{100}$$

For example, if

Gross rate of interest = $4\frac{1}{2}$ per cent

Tax liability $= 30p$ in £

Then

$$\text{Net rate of interest} = \text{Gross rate} \times (1 - x)$$

$$= 4\tfrac{1}{2} \times (1 - \tfrac{30}{100})$$

$$= 4\tfrac{1}{2} \times \tfrac{70}{100}$$

$$= 3.15 \text{ per cent}$$

The net interest rate usually used in the formula is $2\tfrac{1}{2}$ or 3 per cent.
The sinking fund element s must be increased by multiplying by the gross adjustment factor T_G, where

$$T_G = \frac{1}{1 - x}$$

So that the sinking fund element becomes

$$s\left(\frac{1}{1 - x}\right)$$

The adjusted formula is

$$YP = \frac{1}{i + s\left(\dfrac{1}{1 - x}\right)}$$

A problem in ascertaining capital values may be that different investors have differing tax responsibilities. If no specific information is given, it is usual when using the formula to take the basic rate of tax for x. A typical tax rate is 33 per cent.

Example. What is the capital value of an income of £500 per annum receivable for 12 years only? An investor will require an 8 per cent return and a sinking fund could be invested at $4\tfrac{1}{4}$ per cent gross.

$$\text{Net interest for } s = \text{Gross interest} \times (1 - x)$$

$$= 4\tfrac{1}{4} \times (1 - \tfrac{33}{100})$$

$$= 4\tfrac{1}{4} \times \tfrac{67}{100}$$

$$= 2.847 \text{ per cent}$$

(Say, 3 per cent since valuation tables are worked to the nearest $\frac{1}{2}$ per cent.) Then

Net income per annum $= £500$

YP for 12 years at 8 per cent and 3 per cent net (tax 33p in £)

$$= \frac{1}{i + s\left(\dfrac{1}{1-x}\right)}$$

$$= \frac{1}{0.08 + \left(\dfrac{0.03}{1.03^{12} - 1} \times \dfrac{1}{0.67}\right)}$$

$$= \frac{1}{0.08 + \left(0.071 \times \dfrac{1}{0.67}\right)}$$

$$= \frac{1}{0.08 + 0.1059} = \frac{1}{0.1859} \qquad = \underline{5.379}$$

Capital value $= £2690$

This can be checked as follows.

Net income per annum $= £500$

Less s to recoup £2690 in 12 years time at 3 per cent net

$= 0.071 \times 2690 = 190.99$

Tax at 33p in £ on s

$= (0.1059 - 0.071)\, 2690 = 0.0349 \times 2690 = \underline{93.88}$ $\underline{£284.87}$

Spendable income per annum $£215.13$

YP in perpetuity at 8 per cent $= \underline{12.5}$

Capital value $= £2690$

The Annuity £1 will Purchase

This is the annual income receivable at the end of each year for n years if £1 is invested at i compound interest and a sinking fund is provided at $2\frac{1}{2}$ per cent to recoup the £1 at the end of the term. It is the reciprocal of the YP Dual Rate table. Hence

$$\text{Annuity £1 will purchase} = i + s$$

An alternative name is the Annual Equivalent.

Example. A purchaser recently bought an interest for £20 000; it had 15 years' duration. If he required a 7 per cent return, what was the net income per annum receivable from the property?

$$\text{Net income per annum} = \text{Capital value} \times (i + s)$$

$$= 20\,000 \times \left(0.07 + \frac{0.025}{1.025^{15} - 1}\right)$$

$$= 20\,000 \times (0.07 + 0.056)$$

$$= 20\,000 \times 0.126$$

$$= £2520$$

This could have been calculated by dividing the capital value by the YP

$$\frac{£20\,000}{\text{YP for 15 years at 7 per cent and } 2\frac{1}{2} \text{ per cent}}$$

$$= \frac{20\,000}{7.936}$$

$$= £2520$$

There is, also, an Annuity £1 will purchase table on a Single Rate basis. This allows for the sinking fund to accumulate at the same rate as that which is required on the invested capital.

Taking the previous example, if the sinking fund were invested at 7 per cent

$$\text{Net income per annum} = £20\,000 \times (i + s)$$

$$= 20\,000 \times \left(0.07 + \frac{0.07}{1.07^{15} - 1}\right)$$

$$= 20\,000 \times (0.07 + 0.0397)$$

$$= 20\,000 \times 0.1097$$

$$= £2194$$

QUESTIONS

5.7 Calculate the YP Dual Rate for 15 years at 9 per cent and 3 per cent net (tax 33p in £).

5.8 An investor receives an income of £500 per annum from an interest for 25 years only. Calculate the capital value, assuming he requires a yield of 10 per cent. A sinking fund could be invested at 5 per cent gross, and the investor's tax liability is 33p in £.

5.9 An income of £1 per annum receivable for 32 years is worth £8. If a sinking fund can be invested at $2\frac{1}{2}$ per cent net and tax is 40 p in £, what is the yield?

5.10 An income of £750 per annum is receivable for 19 years only. Assuming a yield of 7 per cent and a sinking fund of $2\frac{1}{2}$ per cent net, calculate the capital value of the income if (i) there is no allowance for tax, and (ii) there is an allowance of 40p in £ for tax.

5.11 A purchaser recently bought an interest, which had 10 years' duration, for £12 300. If he required an 8 per cent return, what was the net income per annum receivable from the property? (Ignore tax.)

MORTGAGE INSTALMENT TABLE

This indicates the equal amounts to be paid monthly to redeem each £100 capital borrowed over *n* years at *i* compound interest. It is calculated on a fixed annual basis with no allowance for interest to compound on each monthly instalment.

It is an extension on a Single Rate basis of the Annuity £1 will purchase formula.

The Mortgage Instalment table is computed from

$$\frac{(i + s)\,100}{12}$$

Example. Calculate the monthly instalment to redeem £3000 borrowed over 25 years at $10\frac{1}{2}$ per cent compound interest.

Capital sum per annum = £3000

Mortgage redemption for £3000

$$= 30 \times \frac{(i + s)\,100}{12}$$

$$= 30 \times \frac{\left(0.105 + \dfrac{0.105}{1.105^{25} - 1}\right)100}{12}$$

$$= 30 \times \frac{0.114 \times 100}{12}$$

$$= 30 \times 0.95$$

$$= £28.5 \text{ per month}$$

An alternative formula was used when mortgages were considered in chapter 2. This was

$$P = \frac{M\,(1 + i)^n i}{(1 + i)^n - 1}$$

Taking the previous example

$$P = \frac{3000 \times (1.105)^{25} \times 0.105}{1.105^{25} - 1}$$

$$= \frac{3000 \times 12.16 \times 0.105}{11.16}$$

$$= £343.22 \text{ per annum}$$

This gives a monthly payment of £28.6.

It is possible to calculate the amount of capital outstanding at a particular time by multiplying the annual repayment by the Years' Purchase for the unexpended term of the borrowing period.

Example. In the previous example £3000 was borrowed over 25 years at $10\frac{1}{2}$ per cent, compound interest. The annual repayment was £343.22. What capital would be outstanding after 10 years?

Capital outstanding = Annual repayment $\times$ YP for the
unexpired term

$$343.22 \times \frac{1}{i + s}$$

$$= 343.22 \times \frac{1}{\left(0.105 + \dfrac{0.105}{1.105^{15} - 1}\right)}$$

$$= 343.22 \times \frac{1}{0.105 + 0.0303}$$

$$= 343.22 \times 7.39$$

$$= £2536$$

QUESTIONS

5.12 Calculate the monthly instalments to redeem £2000 to be repaid over 20 years at $8\frac{1}{2}$ per cent compound interest.

5.13 A borrower can afford a mortgage repayment of £25 per month. If he wishes to redeem capital over 18 years at $9\frac{1}{2}$ per cent compound interest what is the maximum amount he can borrow?

VALUATION FORMULAE AND THEIR INTER-RELATIONSHIP

Many examinations in the subject of valuation will include questions designed to test the candidate's knowledge of valuation formulae and how they relate. Such questions may take the following form.

Example. Given that the PV of £1 in 20 years at 5 per cent = 0.377, calculate the YP Single Rate for 20 years at 5 per cent.

The formula for YP Single Rate is

$$\frac{1 - PV}{i}$$

It is given that the PV of £1 for 20 years at 5 per cent is 0.377, hence

$$\text{YP for 20 years at 5 per cent} = \frac{1 - 0.377}{0.05} = \frac{0.623}{0.05}$$

$$= 12.46$$

There may be information given that cannot always be directly substituted into another formula.

Example. Given that the Annual Sinking fund to replace £1 in 21 years at $2\frac{1}{2}$ per cent is 0.037, calculate the Present Value of £1 in 21 years at $2\frac{1}{2}$ per cent.

It can be seen that the Annual Sinking fund cannot be substituted directly into the PV formula to give the required answer. The formulae for the two should be considered and the common factor found.

$$s = \frac{i}{A - 1}$$

and

$$PV = \frac{1}{A}$$

A is the factor common to both formulae, so that the question should be answered thus

Given that s to replace £1 in 21 years at $2\frac{1}{2}$ per cent is 0.037, then

$$0.037 = \frac{i}{A - 1}$$

$$0.037 = \frac{0.025}{A - 1}$$

$$A = \frac{0.025}{0.037} + 1 = 1.68$$

But

$$PV = \frac{1}{A} = \frac{1}{1.68} = 0.595$$

So that

$$PV \text{ of £1 for 21 years at } 2\frac{1}{2} \text{ per cent} = 0.595$$

The answer to this type of example could be found by using the appropriate formula, without reference to the given information. The function of this type of question, however, is to establish how the formulae have been derived and how they are interdependent. Further examples will illustrate this.

Example. Given that the PV of £1 for 10 years at 5 per cent = 0.614, calculate the Amount of £1 per annum for 8 years at 5 per cent.

$$PV = \frac{1}{A}$$

$$\text{Amount of £1 per annum} = \frac{A - 1}{i}$$

So that the common factor is A. PV of £1 = 0.614 = $1/A$, then

$$A \text{ for 10 years at 5 per cent} = \frac{1}{PV}$$

$$= 1.63$$

$$A \text{ for 8 years at 5 per cent} = \frac{A \text{ for 10 years}}{A \text{ for 2 years}}$$

$$= \frac{1.63}{(1 + i)^2} = \frac{1.63}{1.05^2}$$

$$= \frac{1.63}{1.10} = 1.48$$

So that

Amount of £1 per annum for 8 years at 5 per cent

$$= \frac{A - 1}{i} = \frac{1.48 - 1}{0.05} = \frac{0.48}{0.05}$$

$$= 9.6$$

Example. Calculate the PV of £1 in 3 years at 8 per cent, given that the PV of £1 in 1 year at 8 per cent is 0.926 and the Single Rate YP for 2 years at 8 per cent is 1.783.

$$\text{Single Rate YP} = \frac{1 - PV}{i}$$

$$1.783 = \frac{1 - PV \text{ for 2 years at 8 per cent}}{0.08}$$

$$1.783 \times 0.08 = 1 - PV \text{ for 2 years at 8 per cent}$$

$$PV \text{ for 2 years at 8 per cent} = 1 - (1.783 \times 0.08)$$

$$= 1 - 0.14264 = 0.85736 = 0.8574$$

But PV of £1 for 3 years at 8 per cent = PV of £1 for 2 years at 8 per cent $\times$ PV of £1 for 1 year at 8 per cent

$$= 0.8574 \times 0.926$$

$$= 0.7939$$

Example. Given that the Amount of £1 per annum in 45 years at $1\frac{1}{4}$ per cent is 60, calculate the PV of £1 in 45 years at $1\frac{1}{4}$ per cent.

$$\text{Amount of £1 per annum} = \frac{A - 1}{i}$$

$$\text{PV of £1} = \frac{1}{A}$$

So that the common factor is A

$$60 = \frac{A - 1}{0.0125}$$

$$(60 \times 0.0125) + 1 = A$$

$$1.75 = A$$

But PV $= 1/A$, so that

$$\text{PV of £1 for 45 years at } 1\frac{1}{4} \text{ per cent}$$

$$= \frac{1}{1.75} = 0.5715$$

Example. Calculate the YP for 16 years at 10 per cent and 3 per cent, given that the YP Single Rate at 3 per cent for 16 years is 12.561.

$$\text{YP Single Rate} = \frac{1 - PV}{i} \quad \text{But PV} = \frac{1}{A}$$

$$\text{YP Dual Rate} = \frac{1}{i + s} \quad \text{But } s = \frac{i}{A - 1}$$

The method is to derive A from the first formula, and substitute this in s, which is to be used in the second formula.

$$12.561 = \frac{1 - PV}{0.03}$$

$$(12.561 \times 0.03) = 1 - PV$$

$$PV = 1 - (12.561 \times 0.03)$$

$$= 1 - 0.37683$$

$$= 0.62317$$

So that

$$A \text{ for 16 years at 3 per cent} = \frac{1}{0.62317}$$

$$= 1.605$$

$s = i/(A - 1)$ for 16 years at 3 per cent

$$s = \frac{0.03}{1.605 - 1}$$

$$= \frac{0.03}{0.605} = 0.049$$

Substituting in the YP formula $1/(i + s)$

YP for 16 years at 10 per cent and 3 per cent

$$= \frac{1}{0.10 + 0.049}$$

$$= \frac{1}{0.149}$$

$$= 6.711$$

Example. Value an income of £1000 per annum for 10 years at 10 per cent and $2\frac{1}{2}$ per cent net adjusted for tax at 40p in £, given that the Annual Sinking fund to replace £1 in 10 years at $2\frac{1}{2}$ per cent is 0.08925.

s for 10 years at $2\frac{1}{2}$ per cent   = 0.08925

Net income per annum   = £1000

YP for 10 years at 10 per cent and $2\frac{1}{2}$ per cent
(tax 40p in £)

$$= \frac{1}{i + s\left(\frac{1}{1 - x}\right)} = \frac{1}{0.10 + \left(0.08925 \times \frac{1}{0.6}\right)}$$

$$= \frac{1}{0.10 + 0.1487}$$

$$= \frac{1}{0.2487} \qquad = 4.02$$

$$\text{Capital value} \quad = £4020$$

Another type of question may involve the use of algebraic expressions.

Example. If the Amount of £1 in n years at 10 per cent is p, express the Present Value of £1 in $n + 1$ years at 10 per cent in terms of p.

$$A \text{ for } n \text{ years at 10 per cent} = (1 + i)^n = p$$

So that

$$A \text{ for 1 year at 10 per cent} = \sqrt[n]{p}$$

$$PV \text{ for 1 year at 10 per cent} = \frac{1}{\sqrt[n]{p}}$$

Thus

$$PV \text{ for } (n + 1) \text{ years at 10 per cent} = \frac{1}{(\sqrt[n]{p})^{n+1}}$$

Questions may be asked to test a candidate's knowledge of Dual Rate principles and the effect of tax on the sinking fund element and the sinking fund interest.

Example. Your client, Mr Mutt, recently bought at auction an interest in a property yielding £100 per annum net. He paid £1000 for this interest which gives him, he says, a clear 10 per cent return. You happen to know that the interest has only 18 years unexpired term. Calculate for Mr Mutt his true return, correct to two places of decimals, after allowing for a sinking fund at 3 per cent throughout (no allowance for tax).

$$\text{Perpetual interest} = 10 \text{ per cent}$$

So that

$$YP = \frac{1}{i} = \frac{1}{0.10} = 10$$

But income is for 18 years only; thus

$$\text{YP of } 10 = \frac{1}{i+s}$$

$$10 = \frac{1}{i + \dfrac{0.03}{1.03^{18} - 1}}$$

$$10 = \frac{1}{i + 0.0428}$$

$$10(i + 0.0428) = 1$$

$$i = \frac{1 - 0.428}{10}$$

$$= \frac{0.572}{10} = 0.0572$$

$$= 5.72 \text{ per cent}$$

Example. An investor has purchased a leasehold interest in a shop for £6000. The lease has an unexpired term of 15 years and yields a net income of £1000 per annum. Assuming that a sinking fund can be invested at 3 per cent net calculate

    (i) the yield on the investment ignoring the effect of tax on the sinking fund element of the income, and
    (ii) effective yield after allowing for tax at 40p in £.

$$\text{Capital value} = \text{Net income per annum} \times \text{YP}$$

$$£6000 = £1000 \times \text{YP}$$

So that

$$\text{YP} = 6$$

(i) YP for 15 years at *i* and 3 per cent is

$$6 = \frac{1}{i+s}$$

$$= \frac{1}{i + \dfrac{0.03}{1.03^{15} - 1}}$$

$$6 = \frac{1}{i + 0.0538}$$

$$6(i + 0.0538) = 1$$

$$i = \frac{1 - (6 \times 0.0538)}{6}$$

$$= \frac{1 - 0.3228}{6}$$

$$= \frac{0.6722}{6} = 0.1128$$

$$= 11.28 \text{ per cent}$$

(ii) YP for 15 years at i and 3 per cent net (tax 40p in £) is

$$6 = \frac{1}{i + s\left(\frac{1}{1 - x}\right)}$$

$$6 = \frac{1}{i + \left(0.0538 \times \frac{1}{0.6}\right)}$$

$$6 = \frac{1}{i + 0.0897}$$

$$6(i + 0.0897) = 1$$

$$i = \frac{1 - (6 \times 0.0897)}{6}$$

$$= \frac{1 - 0.5382}{6}$$

$$= \frac{0.4618}{6} = 0.077$$

$$= 7.7 \text{ per cent}$$

The following questions are from the examinations of universities and professional bodies and should be used for practice and revision purposes. They should be calculated without the use of valuation tables.

QUESTIONS

5.14 Given that the Amount of £1 per annum in 10 years at 10 per
cent = 15.937 and that $(1.10)^9$ = 2.358, calculate the PV of £1
for 19 years at 10 per cent.

5.15 Given that the Years' Purchase of a reversion to a perpetuity at 10
per cent after 19 years is 1.635, calculate the Annual Sinking fund
to produce £1 in 20 years at 10 per cent.

5.16 Given that the YP in perpetuity at 10 per cent deferred 24 years
is 1.0, calculate the Amount of £1 per annum for 24 years at 10
per cent.

5.17 Given that the Amount of £1 per annum in 6 years at 7 per
cent = 7.153 and that $(1.07)^5$ = 1.403, calculate the PV of £1 for
11 years at 7 per cent.

5.18 Calculate the Annual Sinking fund to replace £1 in 15 years at 6
per cent, given that the PV of £1 in 15 years at 6 per cent = 0.4173.

5.19 Given that the PV of £1 in 47 years at 5 per cent = 0.1, calculate
(i) the Annual Sinking fund to produce £1 in 47 years at 5 per
cent; (ii) the Present Value of £1 per annum in 47 years at 5
per cent. (The result of (i) must not be used to find (ii).)

5.20 Given that the Amount of £1 per annum in 10 years at 4 per
cent = 12, calculate the Years' Purchase for 10 years at 8 per cent
and 4 per cent net, adjusted for tax at 50 per cent.

5.21 Calculate the Annual Sinking fund in 30 years at $5\frac{1}{2}$ per cent,
given that the PV of £1 in 30 years at $5\frac{1}{2}$ per cent is 0.20.

5.22 Calculate the Present Value of £1 per annum in 11 years at 7 per
cent, given that the PV of £1 in 11 years at 7 per cent is 0.475.

5.23 Calculate the Amount of £1 per annum in 20 years at $7\frac{3}{4}$ per cent,
given that the Years' Purchase in 20 years at $7\frac{3}{4}$ per cent is 10.0.

5.24 The Present Value of £y in 8 years at 10 per cent = x. What is the
Amount of £1 per annum in 8 years at 10 per cent in terms of
x and y?

5.25 Explain what the figure of £330 represents in the following calculation

£100 p.a.

Amount of £1 per annum for
6 years at 6 per cent   = 7

X PV of £1 in 6 years at
6 per cent   = 0.7
                                          4.9

X PV of £1 in 7 years at
6 per cent   = 0.67   3.3

£330

5.26 Identify the following resultant figure of 3.337 and show another method of obtaining the same result

Present Value of £1 in 5 years at 6 per cent = 0.7473
Present Value of £1 in 6 years at 6 per cent = 0.7049
Present Value of £1 in 7 years at 6 per cent = 0.6651
Present Value of £1 in 8 years at 6 per cent = 0.6274
Present Value of £1 in 9 years at 6 per cent = 0.5919
                                                                   3.3366

3.337

5.27 A purchaser walked into an auction room and bid 10 YP for a stream of income, believing it to be perpetual. He later discovered that the income only lasts for 25 years. Allowing for a sinking fund for redemption of capital at 4 per cent gross and tax at 25p in £, what will be the real rate of interest he will enjoy?

5.28 The YP at 7 per cent and $2\frac{1}{2}$ per cent gross for 31 years is 10.9, no allowance for tax. Demonstrate how this figure can be arrived at and calculate the corresponding figures

(i) allowing for tax at $62\frac{1}{2}$p in £ on that part of the net income which has to be invested in a sinking fund to redeem the capital only, and then also
(ii) allowing for tax at $37\frac{1}{2}$p in £ on the accumulations of the sinking fund.

5.29 Using a 10 per cent basis, what is the result of investing £1 at the end of each year for a period of 10 years, followed by £2 at the end of each year for the following 10 years?

5.30 £1000 has to be replaced by means of an annual sinking fund over a total period of 10 years. Using a rate of $2\frac{1}{2}$ per cent net and allowing for the fact that the sinking fund in the last five years is to be twice that during the first 5 years what is the annual premium during the first period?

5.31 If, after investing a certain sum of money annually at the end of each of 5 years, and thereafter twice that sum annually at the end of each of the next 5 years, you had accumulated £22 630, what were the annual instalments in each of the 5 year periods respectively, allowing for compound interest throughout the 10 years at 5 per cent?

5.32 Given that the Amount of £1 in 9 years at 8 per cent = 2, calculate the monthly instalment (comprising interest and capital repayment) required to redeem a mortgage loan of £5000 over a period of 10 years at 8 per cent.

5.33 Calculate the capital outstanding on a mortgage of £3000 granted 9 years ago for a period of 10 years at 6 per cent per annum, given that the annual sinking fund to replace £1 in 10 years at 6 per cent is 0.07587.

ADJUSTMENT OF FORMULAE FOR INCOMES OTHER THAN ANNUALLY IN ARREARS

The formulae derived earlier assume that income is received annually at the end of years, and Parry's *Valuation Tables and Conversion Tables* are based upon this assumption.

It is likely that, where property is let, rents will be received in advance, probably on a quarterly basis, and both P. Bowcock and J.J. Rose allow for this in their tables.

The Year's Purchase in perpetuity, shown earlier as $\frac{1}{i}$ may be adjusted by using the following formulae and obtaining the following results.

Assuming a yield of 8 per cent

	Formulae	YP
YP in perpetuity — income annually in advance	$\dfrac{1 + i}{i}$	13.5
YP in perpetuity — income quarterly in advance	$\dfrac{1}{4\left(1 - \sqrt[4]{\dfrac{1}{1+i}}\right)}$	13.119
YP in perpetuity — income quarterly in arrear	$\dfrac{1}{4\left(\sqrt[4]{(1+i)} - 1\right)}$	12.869

If Years' Purchase single rate with income quarterly in advance is required this may be obtained from the formula

$$YP = \frac{\dfrac{1}{4}\left(1 - \dfrac{1}{(1+i)^{n}}\right)}{1 - \sqrt[4]{\dfrac{1}{1+i}}}$$

Example. Calculate the Years' Purchase for 8 years at 8 per cent assuming income quarterly in advance.

$$(1) \quad YP = \frac{\dfrac{1}{4}\left(1 - \dfrac{1}{1.08^{8}}\right)}{1 - \sqrt[4]{\dfrac{1}{1.08}}}$$

$$= \frac{\dfrac{1}{4}(1 - .5403)}{1 - .98094} = 6.03$$

It may not only be Years' Purchase tables which need adjustments for quarterly in advance payments. Sinking fund payments may be required quarterly in advance.

The formula for '*s*' annually in arrears has been proved as $\dfrac{i}{(1+i)^{n} - 1}$

For quarterly in advance, the total annual allowance, s =

$$\frac{4 \times \left(1 - \sqrt[4]{\dfrac{1}{1+i}}\right)}{\left((1+i)^n - 1\right)}$$

Example. Calculate the annual sinking fund to produce £1 in 8 years at 3 per cent, payments quarterly in advance.

$$s = \frac{4 \times 1 - \sqrt[4]{\dfrac{1}{1.03}}}{1.03^8 - 1}$$

$$= 4 \times \frac{1 - .9926}{.2668} = .1109$$

This sinking fund adjustment will be used if the Years' Purchase dual rate with income receivable quarterly in advance and sinking fund payable quarterly in advance is required.

The YP dual rate with tax has been shown as $\dfrac{1}{i + \left[s \text{ net} \left(\dfrac{1}{1-x} \right) \right]}$

This may be adjusted to

$$YP = \frac{1}{4\left[1 - \sqrt[4]{\dfrac{1}{1+i}}\right] + 4\left[\dfrac{1 - \sqrt[4]{\dfrac{1}{1+i}} \times \dfrac{1}{1-x}}{(1+i)^n - 1}\right]}$$

Example. Calculate Years' Purchase for 8 years at 8 per cent and 3 per cent net tax 30p in £, both income and sinking fund quarterly in advance.

$$YP = \frac{1}{4\left[1 - \sqrt[4]{\dfrac{1}{1.08}}\right] + \left(.1109 \times \dfrac{1}{.7}\right)}$$

$$= \frac{1}{(4 \times .0191) + .1584} = 4.259$$

6 THE VALUATION OF FREEHOLD AND LEASEHOLD INTERESTS

It has been shown in chapters 4 and 5 that one method of obtaining the capital value of an interest in property is the Investment Method, namely

Capital value = Net income per annum X Years' Purchase

Net income may be derived from the rent received per annum less outgoings. Years' Purchase will differ according to the yield an investor expects from the property investment; it is suggested that the reader uses the pattern of yields included in chapter 4 as a guide when carrying out valuation exercises.

Once the term of years and yield have been determined, reference can be made to the appropriate table in Parry's *Valuation Tables and Conversion Tables.*

In this chapter, calculations of capital value will be assessed to the nearest £50.

FREEHOLD INTERESTS

The tables normally used for the valuation of freehold interests are

(i) Years' Purchase Single Rate
(ii) Present Value of £1
(iii) Years' Purchase of a Reversion to a Perpetuity

The method may differ according to whether the net income is perpetual, variable or deferred.

Perpetual Income

Property may be let on full repairing and insuring terms at a rent which is equivalent to rack rental value, the lease having no provisions for regular rent reviews. In these circumstances, it may be assumed that the rent will be receivable in perpetuity.

Example. A freehold shop in a provincial town centre has recently been let on full repairing and insuring terms at a rack rent of £5000 per annum. Value the freehold interest.

Assuming a freehold yield on rack rental value terms of 7 per cent

Net income per annum	= £5000
YP in perpetuity at 7 per cent	= 14.286
Capital value	=£71 430
(say)	£71 500

A lease may provide for regular rent reviews, the rent revision to be calculated at the time of the review. This amount cannot be predetermined when valuing the freehold interest, and so the rent reviews are recognised by adjusting the yield.

Example. Modern freehold office premises are let on internal repairing terms at a rent of £5000 per annum. The lease provides for rent reviews at 5-yearly intervals. Value the freehold interest.

Assuming a freehold yield on rack rental value terms of 6 per cent

Rent received per annum		£5000
Less		
External repairs and insurance say 15 per cent of rack rent = £750		
Management say 5 per cent of rack rent	= £250	£1000
Net income per annum		£4000
YP in perpetuity at 6 per cent	=	16.667
Capital value	=	£66 668
(say)		£66 650

Varying and Deferred Incomes

In many freehold interests, the annual income will vary because an existing lease will expire after a known period. The rent being paid may not be the current rack rental value, because it was agreed at some date in the past, and since then values have increased.

Example. A freehold shop in a good trading position is let on full repairing and insuring terms at a rent of £5000 per annum, the lease having 5 years unexpired. The current net rack rental value is £10 000 per annum. Value the freehold interest.

There are two different rents to be capitalised, namely (i) £5000 per annum receivable for 5 years only (the unexpired period of the lease) and (ii) £10 000 per annum receivable in perpetuity, but deferred 5 years (the reversion). It may be considered that the £5000 per annum is secure income, because the tenant is paying a rent, which is half of the full rental value. (The £5000 per annum is said to be *twice secured*.) Hence, the tenant will attempt to comply with all the terms of the lease, so that he does not jeopardise his occupation and the considerable profit rent which he enjoys. Because of the security, the freehold yield on rack rental terms adopted for the reversion may be reduced by, say, 1 per cent for the unexpired period.

It should be emphasised, however, that the position may be different in the case of a long unexpired term and a fixed income. The benefit of security will be cancelled out by the disadvantage of receiving fixed income over a long period, with no protection against inflation.

The appropriate calculation follows, assuming a freehold yield on rack rental value terms to be 7 per cent.

Unexpired term of lease is 5 years

Rent received per annum	= £5000
YP for 5 years at 6 per cent	= 4.212

$$\text{£21 060}$$

Reversion

Net rack rental value per annum = £10 000

YP in perpetuity at 7 per cent
deferred 5 years   = 10.186
                                                              £101 860

                          Capital value   =   £122 920

                                   (say)   £122 900

(*Note* The figure of 10.186 is obtained from the Years' Purchase of a
Reversion to a Perpetuity table.)

A second reason for variations in annual income is that the lease may
incorporate rent reviews, with the amount to be paid at each review
period agreed at the commencement of the lease.

Example. Freehold office premises were let 4 years ago on a full repairing
and insuring lease for a period of 14 years. It was agreed that the rent for
the first 7 years would be £5000 per annum, and for the second 7 years,
£6000 per annum. The current net rack rental value is £7000 per annum.
Value the freehold interest.

This valuation has three different rents to be capitalised, namely

(i)   £5000 per annum receivable for 3 years only,
(ii) £6000 per annum receivable for 7 years only but deferred
3 years, and
(iii) £7000 per annum receivable in perpetuity, but deferred 10
years.

As in the previous example, the rents received under the lease may be
considered to be slightly more secure than the rack rental value, and the
yield adjusted accordingly.

The capital value of the £6000 per annum may be obtained by multiplying the rent per annum by a deferred Years' Purchase. This is obtained
by multiplying together the YP for the period of receipt (7 years) and
the PV of £1 for the period of deferment (3 years).

The appropriate calculation follows assuming a freehold yield on
rack rental value terms to be 6 per cent.

Unexpired term of lease is 3 years

Rent received per annum	= £5000	
YP for 3 years at 5 per cent	= 2.723	
		£13 615

7 years

Rent received per annum	= £6000	
YP for 7 years at 5 per cent	= 5.786	
PV of £1 in 3 years at 5 per cent	= 0.864	
YP for 7 years at 5 per cent deferred 3 years	= 4.999	
		£29 994

Reversion

Net rack rental value per annum	= £7000	
YP in perpetuity at 6 per cent deferred 10 years	= 9.307	£65 149
Capital value	=	£108 758
(say)		£108 750

The deferment of Years' Purchase may be undertaken by either of two methods.

   (i) By multiplying together the YP for the period of receipt and the PV of £1 for the period of deferment (as illustrated in the previous example); or
   (ii) Deduct the YP for the period of deferment from the YP for the period from the time of valuation to the time of expiration of the income The two methods may be illustrated by an example.

Example. £1000 per annum is to be received from a letting of freehold agricultural land for a period of 15 years commencing in 10 years' time. What is the capital value of this annual income?

Assuming a freehold yield on rack rental value terms to be 5 per cent and using (i)

Rent received per annum		= £1000
YP for 15 years at 5 per cent	= 10.380	
PV of £1 in 10 years at 5 per cent	= 0.614	
YP for 15 years at 5 per cent deferred 10 years		= 6.373
	Capital value	= £6373
	(say)	£6350

using (ii)

Rent received per annum		= £1000
YP for 25 years at 5 per cent	= 14.094	
Less YP for 10 years at 5 per cent	= 7.722	
YP for 15 years at 5 per cent deferred 10 years		= 6.372
	Capital value	= £6372
	(say)	£6350

The first method is usually adopted, because it may also be applied to Dual Rate situations (see later in this chapter).

There may be instances where the unexpired period of a lease is very long. In these cases, it may be more practical to treat the income as perpetual, if it is fixed throughout the period of the lease.

Example. Land has been let at a ground rent of £500 per annum, the ground lease having 50 years unexpired. Factory premises have been built on the site, having a current net rack rental value of £2000 per annum. Value the freehold interest, assuming that the freehold yield for a ground rent with a long unexpired term and fixed income is 15 per cent, and for factory premises let on rack rental value terms (but long wait for reversion) is 12 per cent.

Ground lease is 50 years

Rent received per annum	= £500	
YP for 50 years at 15 per cent	= 6.6605	
		£3330

Reversion

Net rack rental value per annum	= £2000	
YP in perpetuity at 12 per cent deferred 50 years	= 0.029	
		£ 58
	Capital value	£3388
	(say)	£3400

Alternatively, the ground rent may be treated as being perpetual and the reversionary income ignored.

Rent received per annum	= £500	
YP in perpetuity at 15 per cent	= 6.667	
	Capital value =	£3333
	(say)	£3350

Circumstances may exist where a building is reaching the end of its physical and economic life. Because of present-day statutory restrictions, the site may not be suitable for further building and will be virtually worthless after the demolition of the existing building. The interest in the land may be freehold, but the income from the building will cease at some future date. Hence, the valuation will require the use of Dual Rate tables (see chapter 5)

Example. A freehold factory, giving a net income of £1000 will be demolished in 10 years' time. The site is not suitable for rebuilding. Value the freehold interest.

Assuming a yield of 14 per cent (old factory premises) and a tax liability of 40p in £

Net income per annum	= £1000
YP for 10 years at 14 per cent and	

$2\frac{1}{2}$ per cent net (tax 40p in £)　　　= 3.463

Capital value　= £3463

(say)　　　　　£3450

By using Dual Rate tables having a sinking fund at $2\frac{1}{2}$ per cent net, provision has been made for the capital sum of £3463 to be available at the end of the 10 year term.

A tax rate of 40p in £ has been used in the above example; tax rates may fluctuate, and the reader should use the rate operative at the time of assessing capital value.

LEASEHOLD INTERESTS

The tables normally used for the valuation of leasehold interests are

(i) Years' Purchase Dual Rate adjusted for tax (throughout the calculations a tax rate of 40p in £ will be used); and
(ii) Present Value of £1.

The valuation may differ according to whether or not the net income or profit rent at the time of valuation is fixed throughout the term of the lease, or is variable or is deferred.

If the property is sublet by the lessee then net income is capitalised; if the lessee occupies the property, then profit rent is capitalised.

Fixed Income for the Period of the Lease

If premises are let on lease at a fixed rent throughout the period of the lease, and the lessee sublets also at a fixed rent, then net income will be constant throughout the lease.

Example. A shop was let on a full repairing and insuring lease at a rent of £1000·per annum, the lease having 8 years unexpired. The premises have been sublet on the same terms at a rent of £1250 per annum, the sublease expiring 3 days before the main lease. The current net rack rental value is £1600 per annum. Value the leasehold and subleasehold interests.

Assuming a freehold yield on rack rental value terms to be 7 per cent, then a leasehold interest involves greater risk and an appropriate yield would be 8 per cent. The subleasehold may be $8\frac{1}{2}$ per cent. Tax liability is 40p in £.

Leasehold Interest

Rent received per annum		= £1250
Less Rent paid per annum		= £1000
Net income per annum		= £250
YP for 8 years at 8 per cent and $2\frac{1}{2}$ per cent net (tax 40p in £)		= 3.693
Capital value		= £ 923
(say)		£ 900

Subleasehold Interest

Net rack rental value per annum		= £1600
Less Rent paid per annum		= £1250
Profit rent per annum		= £ 350
YP for 8 years at $8\frac{1}{2}$ per cent and $2\frac{1}{2}$ per cent net (tax 40p in £)		= 3.626
Capital value		= £1269
(say)		£1250

Varying and Deferred Incomes during the Period of the Lease

The net income to be capitalised may vary for two reasons

(i) The rent to be paid to the freeholder or lessor may be regularly reviewed during the period of the lease, and/or

(ii) the rent received from a sublessee may be reviewed during the sublease period.

In the case of an occupying lessee or sublessee, the profit rent may vary because of rent reviews.

Example. Office premises have been let by the freeholder on a full
repairing and insuring lease, the lease having 14 years unexpired; the
rent to be paid for the next 7 years is £1000 per annum and for the
7 years thereafter is £1250 per annum. The premises have been sublet,
the sublease expiring 3 days before the main lease; the rent to be paid
for the next 7 years is £1350 per annum and for the 7 years thereafter
is £1550 per annum. The current net rack rental value is £1750 per
annum. Value the leasehold and subleasehold interests.

Leasehold interest This valuation has two different net incomes, namely

   (i) £350 per annum (£1350 − £1000) receivable for 7 years and
   (ii) £300 per annum (£1550 − £1250) receivable for 7 years, but
deferred 7 years.

The £300 per annum is capitalised by a deferred YP. This is obtained by
multiplying together the YP for the period of receipt and the PV of £1
for the period of deferment. Thus, assuming a leasehold yield to be 7
per cent (1 per cent more than freehold yield on rack rental value terms),
and a tax liability of 40p in £

First 7 Years

Rent received per annum	= £1350
Less Rent paid per annum	= £1000
Net income per annum	= £ 350
YP for 7 years at 7 per cent and $2\frac{1}{2}$ per cent net (tax 40p in £)	= 3.438
	£1203

Second 7 Years

Rent received per annum	= £1550
Less Rent paid per annum	= £1250
Net income per annum	= £ 300
YP for 7 years at 7 per cent and $2\frac{1}{2}$ per cent net (tax 40p in £) = 3.438	
PV of £1 in 7 years at 7 per cent = 0.623	

YP for 7 years at 7 per cent and
$2\frac{1}{2}$ per cent (tax 40p in £)
deferred 7 years   = 2.142

	643
Capital value	= £1846
(say)	£1850

Subleasehold interest This valuation has two differing amounts of profit rent, namely

  (i) £400 per annum (£1750 − £1350) receivable for 7 years and
  (ii) £200 per annum (£1750 − £1550) receivable for 7 years, but deferred 7 years.

Assuming a subleasehold yield of $7\frac{1}{2}$ per cent ($\frac{1}{2}$ per cent more than leasehold) and a tax liability of 40p in £

First 7 Years

Net rack rental value per annum	= £1750
Less Rent paid per annum	= £1350
Profit rent per annum	= £ 400

YP for 7 years at $7\frac{1}{2}$ per cent and $2\frac{1}{2}$
per cent net (tax 40p in £)   = 3.380

                                                              £1352

Second 7 Years

Net rack rental value per annum	= £1750
Less Rent paid per annum	= £1550
Profit rent per annum	= £ 200

YP for 7 years at $7\frac{1}{2}$ per
cent and $2\frac{1}{2}$ per cent net
(tax 40p in £)   = 3.380

PV of £1 in 7 years at
$7\frac{1}{2}$ per cent   = 0.603

YP for 7 years at $7\frac{1}{2}$ per cent and
$2\frac{1}{2}$ per cent net (tax 40p in £)
deferred 7 years   = 2.038

$$£ \underline{\ 408}$$

Capital value	= £1760
(say)	£1750

Non-tax-paying Investors

Some investors such as charities have complete or partial exemption from tax-paying commitments. These investors will be attracted by short-term leasehold interests, because they will not have to take tax into account when setting aside a sinking fund to recoup the capital used to purchase the property.

Example. A property, let on a full repairing and insuring lease having 10 years unexpired, provides a net income of £1000 per annum. An investor could expect a yield of 7 per cent. Assuming an investor has a tax liability of 40p in £, then he could afford to purchase the interest at a price calculated as follows

Net income per annum	= £1000
YP for 10 years at 7 per cent and $2\frac{1}{2}$ per cent net (tax 40p in £)	= $\underline{\ 4.571}$
Capital value	= £4571
(say)	£4550

If the investor is exempt from tax liabilities, he can afford to purchase the interest at a price calculated as follows.

A sinking fund of $2\frac{1}{2}$ per cent net was used in the previous calculation. The non-tax-paying investor, however, can provide a sinking fund at the gross rate of interest, namely

Net rate X Gross adjustment factor

that is

$$2\frac{1}{2} \times \frac{1}{1-x} \quad \left(\text{where } x = \frac{\text{tax rate in new pence}}{100}\right)$$

$$= 2\frac{1}{2} \times \frac{1}{1 - 0.40}$$

$$= 2\frac{1}{2} \times \frac{1}{0.60}$$

$$= 4.167 \text{ per cent}$$

$$(\text{say}) = 4\frac{1}{4} \text{ per cent}$$

(Annual Sinking Fund tables to $\frac{1}{4}$ per cent intervals) Then

Net income per annum $= £1000$

YP for 10 years at 7 per cent and
$4\frac{1}{4}$ per cent gross $=$

$$\frac{1}{i+s} = \cfrac{1}{0.07 + \cfrac{0.0425}{1.0425^{10} - 1}}$$

$$= \frac{1}{0.07 + 0.0823} \qquad = \underline{6.566}$$

$$\text{Capital value} \qquad = \underline{£6566}$$

$$(\text{say}) \qquad = \underline{£6550}$$

The non-tax-paying investor could obtain a 7 per cent yield by purchasing the interest for £6566, whereas investors paying tax at 40p in £ could only afford to pay £4571.

If the non-tax-paying investor is in competition with other investors, all having tax liabilities, he may purchase the interest by over-bidding his competitors, at a purchase price of say £5000. Hence, he would obtain a greater yield than 7 per cent. This may be calculated as follows

$$\text{YP} = \frac{\text{Purchase Price}}{\text{Net income per annum}} = \frac{£5000}{£1000} = 5$$

YP for 10 years at i per cent
and $4\frac{1}{4}$ per cent gross $= 5$

$$5 = \frac{1}{i + 0.0823}$$

$$i = \frac{1 - (5 \times 0.0823)}{5}$$

$$= \frac{1 - 0.4115}{5} = \frac{0.5885}{5}$$

$$= 0.1177$$

$$= 11\frac{3}{4} \text{ per cent}$$

PROFIT RENT

Profit rent per annum is the difference between the rack rental value per annum and the rent paid per annum by an occupying lessee or sublessee on the same repairing and insuring terms.

Where a profit rent exists, the occupier has a saving on his annual expenses because he pays less for his occupation than the full rental value. This situation may occur because the lessee or sublessee has been in occupation for a period of time and his rent has not been reviewed recently, or he may have paid a premium at the commencement or during the period of his lease (see next section). When an occupier wishes to sell his lease or sublease, the profit rent per annum is capitalised to arrive at capital value.

Example. A shop is let on full repairing and insuring terms at a rent of £1200 per annum, the lease having 12 years unexpired. The net rack rental value is £1500 per annum. Value the leasehold interest.

Assuming a yield of 7 per cent and a tax liability of 40p in £

	Net rack rental value per annum		= £1500
Less	Rent paid per annum		= £1200
	Profit rent per annum		= £ 300
	YP for 12 years at 7 per cent and $2\frac{1}{2}$ per cent (tax 40p in £)		= 5.241
	Capital value		= £1572
		(say)	£1550

The comparison between rack rental value and the rent paid must be made, when both are in relation to the same repairing and insuring terms. For example, it would be incorrect to compare a rent paid under an internal repairing lease with a net rack rental value; the rack rental value should be adjusted to internal repairing terms. Table 6.1 illustrates how the rack rental value alters according to differing repairing responsibilities incorporated in leases. The total annual cost to the tenant of rack rent and repair and insurance payments will be the same, irrespective of the division of repair and insurance responsibility.

Table 6.1   *Calculation of Rack Rental Value in Relation to Differing Repair and Insurance Responsibilities*

Assume that premises have a net rack rental value of £1000 per annum; it is estimated that external repairs will cost £100 per annum, internal repairs £50 per annum and insurance £5 per annum.

The table illustrates how the rack rental value of the premises varies, according to differing repair and insurance responsibilities.

	Tenant is responsible for all repairs and insurance	Tenant has no respons- ibility for repairs and insurance	Tenant is responsible for external repairs and insurance only	Tenant is responsible for internal repairs only
Rack rental value per annum	£1000	£1155	£1050	£1105
Cost of external repairs per annum	£ 100	–	£ 100	–
Cost of internal repairs per annum	£ 50	–	–	£ 50
Cost of insurance per annum	£ 5	–	£ 5	–
Total cost to the tenant per annum of rent, repairs and insurance	£1155	£1155	£1155	£1155

Example. Premises are let on an internal repairing lease at £1000 per annum. The net rack rental value is £1200 per annum. Calculate the profit rent per annum.

The rack rental value is £1200 per annum, when the tenant is responsible for all repairs and insurance. If the tenant is responsible for internal repairs only he would expect to pay a higher rent than £1200, namely £1200 plus external repairs and insurance (those items for which he is not responsible under the internal repairing lease). Thus adjusted rack rental value per annum = net rack rental value + cost of external repairs and insurance (say $12\frac{1}{2}$ per cent of net rack rental value) = £1200 + £150 = £1350 per annum

Adjusted rack rental value per annum	= £1350
Less Rent paid per annum on the same terms	= £1000
Profit rent per annum	= £ 350

PREMIUMS

A premium is a sum of money that is paid by a lessee at the commence-ment, or during the period, of a lease in consideration of a reduction in rent. The lessee purchases an annual profit rent and the landlord capitalises a part of his future income. The landlord receives a capital sum for immediate investment, which may be partially tax-free, and the security of his annual income is increased. The premium may have the effect of increasing the landlord's confidence in his tenant where consents are required under the lease, such as permission to alter or improve the premises.

Calculation of the Premium or Reduction in Rent

A lessee may request a specified deduction in rent per annum upon the granting of a lease; the premium to be paid should be equivalent to the capital value of the annual profit rent.

Example. A lessee has been granted a 14-year lease of a shop having a net rack rental value of £1500 per annum. He has agreed to pay £1000 per annum, subject to the immediate payment of a premium. Calculate the premium.

Assuming a yield of 7 per cent and a tax liability of 40p in £

Net rack rental value per annum	= £1500
Less Rent to be paid per annum	= £1000
Profit rent per annum	= £ 500
YP for 14 years at 7 per cent and $2\frac{1}{2}$ per cent net (tax 40p in £)	= 5.852
Premium	= £2926

Alternatively the premium may be agreed and the reduction in rent per annum has to be calculated. The lessee will forego a capital sum, and he will expect in return a reduction in rent totalling

(i) the interest foregone on the premium at the leasehold rate of interest, *i* and

(ii) a sum sufficient to recover the initial capital outlay by means of a sinking fund (adjusted for tax liabilities) at the time the lease expires, $s(1/1 - x)$, so that the total is

$$i + s\left(\frac{1}{1 - x}\right)$$

This is the annual equivalent of the premium, or the Annuity £1 will Purchase (see chapter 5).

The reduction in rent may be calculated as

Premium X Annuity £1 will purchase

or more conveniently

$$\frac{\text{Premium}}{\text{YP for the term of the lease}}$$

Example. A shop is to be let on a 14-year full repairing and insuring lease having a net rack rental value of £1200 per annum. The tenant has agreed to pay a premium of £2000 at the commencement of the lease. Calculate the rent per annum to be paid. Assuming a yield of 7 per cent and a tax liability of 40p in £

Net rack rental value per annum   = £1200

Less Reduction in rent

Annual equivalent of the premium

$= \dfrac{2000}{\begin{array}{c}\text{YP for 14 years at 7 per cent and}\\ 2\frac{1}{2} \text{ per cent net (tax 40p in £)}\end{array}}$

$= \dfrac{2000}{5.852}$ = £ 342

Rent to be paid per annum   = £ 858

There may be instances where the tenant agrees to pay a premium at a future date. In order to calculate the reduction in rent per annum, the present cost of the future premium may be determined and the annual equivalent then found.

Example. A tenant has been granted a 14-year full repairing and insuring lease of premises having a net rack rental value per annum of £2000. The tenant has agreed to pay a premium of £3000 in 5 years' time. Calculate the rent per annum he should pay, assuming a yield of 8 per cent and a tax liability of 40p in £.

Net rack rental value per annum   = £2000

Less Reduction in rent

Present cost of premium =

£3000 × PV of £1 in 5 years at $2\frac{1}{2}$ per cent

= £3000 × 0.884 = £2652

Annual equivalent = $\dfrac{£2652}{\text{YP for 14 years at 8 per cent and } 2\frac{1}{2} \text{ per cent net (tax 40p in £)}}$

$= \dfrac{£2652}{5.528}$ = £480

Rent to be paid per annum   = £1520

Where a tenant has a liability to pay a premium at a known future date, he may provide for this by investing a capital sum or by an annual sinking fund. In either case, the rate of interest for investment to provide the capital sum should be a low risk-free rate, that is, an accumulative rate of interest such as $2\frac{1}{2}$ or 3 per cent net.

Example. Considering the previous example, where a tenant agreed to pay a premium of £3000 in 5 years' time, this may be provided by investment of an initial capital sum or an annual sinking fund.

(i) Initial capital sum = £3000 × PV of £1 in 5 years at $2\frac{1}{2}$ per cent

= £3000 × 0.884 = £2652

(ii) Annual sinking fund = £3000 × Annual sinking fund to provide £1 in 5 years at $2\frac{1}{2}$ per cent

= £3000 × 0.190 = £570

Note The value of the future premium to the landlord at the commencement of the lease is £3000 deferred by a remunerative rate of interest; that is, £3000 × PV of £1 in 5 years at 8 per cent = £3000 × 0.681 = £2043. It is usual, however, to calculate the premium or rent from the tenant's viewpoint.

COMBINED FREEHOLD AND LEASEHOLD VALUATIONS

A characteristic of land and property is that there may exist at the same time freehold, leasehold and subleasehold interests, all having capital values. A valuer may be required to calculate the value of each of these interests.

Example. Brown is the freeholder of a shop let to Black at £1000 per annum, the lease having 13 years unexpired. Black pays rates and is responsible for internal repairs only. Brown pays the fire insurance, and has responsibility for external repairs. Black sublet to Green last year for a period of 7 years at a rent of £1500 per annum and a premium of £1000. Green holds on the same terms as Black as regards outgoings. The current net rack rental value is £2500 per annum. Value the interests of Brown, Black and Green and show the maximum amount that Green can afford to pay for the interests of Brown and Black.

Brown's interest Assuming a freehold yield on rack rental value terms to be 7 per cent

Unexpired term of lease is 13 years

Rent received per annum	= £1000	
Less External repairs and insurance say $7\frac{1}{2}$ per cent of net rack rent		
£2500	= £ 187	
Net income per annum	= £ 813	
YP for 13 years at 6 per cent	= 8.853	
		£7197

Reversion

Net rack rental value per annum	= £2500
YP in perpetuity deferred 13 years	
at 7 per cent	= 5.928

		£14 820
Capital value	=	£22 017
(say)		£22 000

Black's interest Assume leasehold yield to be 8 per cent on rack rental value terms and tax liability to be 40p in £.

First 6 years

Rent received per annum	= £1500
Less Rent paid per annum	= £1000
Net income per annum	= £ 500
YP for 6 years at 7 per cent and $2\frac{1}{2}$ per cent net (tax 40p in £)	= 3.022
	£1511

Second 7 years

Reversion to adjusted rack rental value per annum
(Under the main lease Black is responsible for internal repairs only, so that this is the only repair liability he would impose on a sublessee) Hence

Adjusted rack rental value per annum =

£2500 + external repairs + insurance =
£2500 + £187   = £2687

Less Rent paid per annum   = £1000

Net income per annum   = £1687

YP for 7 years at 8 per cent and $2\frac{1}{2}$ per cent net (tax 40p in £) = 3.324

PV of £1 in 6 years at 8 per cent   = 0.630

YP for 7 years at 8 per cent and $2\frac{1}{2}$ per cent net (tax 40p in £) deferred 6 years = 2.094

£3532

	Capital value	= £5043
	(say)	£5050

Green's interest

Assume subleasehold yield to be $8\frac{1}{2}$ per cent and tax liability to be 40p in £.

Adjusted rack rental value per annum	= £2687
Less Rent paid per annum	= £1500
Profit Rent per annum	= £1187
YP for 6 years at $8\frac{1}{2}$ per cent and $2\frac{1}{2}$ per cent net (tax 40p in £)	= 2.891
Capital value	= £3432
(say)	£3450

Note

(i) The premium of £1000 has been paid a year ago, and has no relevance to the calculation of capital value at the present time.

(ii) Rates do not appear in the calculation because it is a common item to both the adjusted rack rental value and the rent paid.

If Green purchased the interests of Brown and Black, he would have an unencumbered freehold interest, the value being

Net rack rental value per annum	= £2500
YP in perpetuity at 7 per cent	= 14.286
Capital value	= £35 715
(say)	£35 700

He could afford to pay for Brown's and Black's interests £35 700 less the Value of the lease he forfeits, that is £35 700 − £3450 = £32 250. Other investors would expect to pay £27 050 (£22 000 + £5050), because they would be buying subject to the lease and sublease. Green has £5200 (£32 250 − £27 050) which he can use to outbid his competitors. This may be apportioned as the capital values of Brown's and Black's interest. So that the maximum amounts he can afford to pay for the interests are

Brown's interest

$$£22\,000 + £(5200 \times \frac{22\,000}{27\,050})$$

$$= £22\,000 + £4230$$

$$= £26\,230$$

(say) £26 250

Black's interest

$$£5050 + £(5200 \times \frac{5050}{27\,050})$$

$$= £5050 + £970$$

$$= £6020$$

(say) £6000

Example. X is the freeholder of shop premises worth a net rack rental value of £2500 per annum. 30 years ago, X let the premises on ground lease to Y for 99 years at a rent of £100 per annum. 11 years ago, Y sublet the whole to Z for 21 years at a rent of £1000 per annum, Z being responsible for internal repairs and rates. Value the interests of X, Y and Z.

X's interest Assuming that the freehold yield for a ground rent with long unexpired term and fixed income is 12 per cent, and that the ground rent is virtually perpetual.

Ground rent per annum	= £	100
YP in perpetuity at 12 per cent	=	8.333
Capital value	= £	833
(say)	£	850

Y's interest Assuming a leasehold yield of 7 per cent and tax liability of 40p in £.

Unexpired term of sublease is 10 years

Rent received per annum		= £1000
Less Ground rent per annum	= £100	

External repairs and
insurance (say $7\frac{1}{2}$ per cent
of net rack rent £2500)   £187

	£ 287
Net income per annum =	713

YP for 10 years at 6 per cent and
$2\frac{1}{2}$ per cent net (tax 40p in £)   = 4.790

$$£3415$$

Remaining 59 years

Reversion to net rack rental value
per annum   = £2500

Less Ground rent per annum   = £ 100

Net income per annum   = £2400

YP for 59 years at 7 per cent and
$2\frac{1}{2}$ per cent net (tax 40p
in £)   12.098

PV of £1 in 10 years at
7 per cent   = 0.508

YP for 59 years at 7 per cent and $2\frac{1}{2}$
per cent net (tax 40p in £) deferred
10 years   = 6.146   £14 750

Capital value   = £18 165

(say)   £18 150

Z's interest Assuming a subleasehold yield of 8 per cent and tax liability
of 40p in £.

Adjusted rack rental value per annum = Net rack rental value +
external repairs + insurance = 2500 + 187 = £2687

Less Rent paid per annum   = £1000

Profit Rent per annum   = £1687

YP for 10 years at 8 per cent and
$2\frac{1}{2}$ per cent net (tax 40p in £)   = 4.371

Capital value   = £7374

(say)   £7350

The questions at the end of this chapter are taken from the examinations of universities, polytechnics and professional bodies and should be used for practice and revision purposes.

DOUBLE SINKING FUND

The valuation of variable incomes from terminable interests such as leasehold was described earlier in this chapter. The following example illustrates the approach.

Example. Premises are let on a full repairing and insuring lease having 15 years unexpired at a rent of £200 per annum. The premises are sublet on the same terms at a rent of £300 per annum, the sublease having 5 years unexpired. The net rack rental value per annum is £400 per annum. Value the leasehold interest.

Assuming a leasehold yield on rack rental value terms of 8 per cent and a tax liability of 40p in £.

First 5 years

	Rent received per annum	= £300	
Less	Rent paid per annum	= £200	
	Net income per annum	= £100	
	YP for 5 years at 7 per cent and $2\frac{1}{2}$ per cent net (tax 40p in £)	= 2.583	
			£258

Second 10 years

	Net rack rental value per annum	= £400
Less	Rent paid per annum	= £200
	Net income per annum	= £200
	YP for 10 years at 8 per cent and $2\frac{1}{2}$ per cent net (tax 40p in £)	= 4.371
	PV of £1 in 5 years at 8 per cent	= 0.681
	YP for 10 years at 8 per cent and $2\frac{1}{2}$ per cent net (tax 40p in £) deferred 5 years	= 2.977

$$£595$$

$$\text{Capital value} \quad = \quad £853$$

This method is commonly used for the valuation of terminable interests, and its accuracy may be questioned. It may be slightly incorrect because it provides for more than one sinking fund being taken out to redeem capital, whereas in all probability the purchaser would take out a single policy to cover the whole term. The traditional approach is made in two stages, so that in the previous example each separate sinking fund is based on 5 years and 10 years respectively, not over 15 years, the full period of the unexpired term. This may be overcome by using the Double Sinking Fund Method. Considering the previous example, let Capital value = P

First 5 Years

Rent received per annum	= £300
Less Rent paid per annum	= £200
Net income per annum	= £100

Less s to replace P in 15 years at $2\frac{1}{2}$ per cent net (tax 40p in £)

$$= (0.056 \times \frac{1}{1-x}) \times P$$

$$= (0.056 \times \frac{1}{0.6}) \times P \qquad = 0.093P$$

Spendable income per annum	= £100 − 0.093P
YP (Single rate) for 5 years at 7 per cent	= 4.100

$$£410 - 0.381P$$

Second 10 years

Net rack rental value per annum	= £400
Less Rent paid per annum	= £200
Net income per annum	= £200
Less Sinking Fund as before	= 0.093P
Spendable income per annum	= £200 − 0.093P

YP for 10 years at 8 per
cent   = 6.710

PV of £1 in 5 years at
8 per cent   = 0.681

YP for 10 years at 8 per
cent deferred 5 years   − 4.569

$$\frac{£\ 914 - 0.425P}{£1324 - 0.806P}$$

Plus

*Repayment of capital replaced
by single rate sinking fund P

PV of £1 in 5 years at
7 per cent   = 0.713

PV of £1 in 10 years
at 8 per cent   = 0.463 = 0.330   0.330P

Capital value   = £1324 − 0.476P

But capital value = P

$P = 1324 - 0.476P$

$1.476P = £1324$

$P = \dfrac{1324}{1.476}$

= £897

*The capital has been replaced twice, at the accumulative rate of $2\frac{1}{2}$ per cent net (taxed) which is correct, and also at the rates of 7 per cent and 8 per cent, because the Single Rate tables have a built-in sinking fund. The capital value of the interest has been excessively reduced, so that the deferred capital value is added back.

The Double Sinking Fund method indicates a difference of £44 in this example using the normal method which is equivalent to 5 per cent.

However, in the majority of leasehold valuations the traditional method continues to be used.

6.1   *A* is the freeholder of old factory premises let to *B* 69 years ago on
a 99-year ground lease at a rent of £100 per annum. *B* sublet the
premises to *C* 15 years ago for 21 years at a rent of £700 per annum
with *B* liable only for structural repairs and insurance. The present
rental value on the same terms is £1500 per annum. Value the
interests of *A*, *B* and *C*.

6.2   A small modern office building well situated in the centre of a city
is occupied by the head lessee on a lease having 49 years unexpired
at a ground rent of £400 per annum. The current net rack rental
value is £3000 per annum. The freeholder has decided to sell his
interest.
(i) Value the freehold interest assuming the lessees will not buy.
(ii) What is the maximum amount the lessee can afford to pay for
the freehold, assuming he wishes to purchase it?

6.3   James is the freeholder of a town house worth a net rack rental
value of £700 per annum exclusive. 34 years ago, he let to John on
a 99 year ground lease at a rent of £100 per annum. 7 years ago,
John sublet to Jane on a 21-year lease at a rent of £400 per annum
exclusive, John being responsible for external repairs and insurance,
Jane for the remainder of the outgoings. 5 years ago, Jane sublet to
Jill for 7 years at a rent of £600 per annum exclusive, Jill having no
responsibility for repairs. Value all interests.

6.4   *X* is the owner of a freehold interest in a shop which has a current
net rack rental value of £1200 per annum. 14 years ago, *X* let the
shop to *Y* on a 21-year lease on full repairing and insuring terms at
a rent of £400 per annum, subject to a premium of £1500. 11 years
ago, *Y* sublet the premises to *Z* on a 14-year lease at £700 per
annum with *Z* responsible for internal repairs and insurance. *Z*
paid a premium of £500. The shop is in need of external repairs
and it is estimated that these will cost £200. Value the interests of
X, *Y* and *Z*.

6.5   5 years ago, a small modern freehold factory was let on a 21-year
full repairing and insuring lease. The lessee is liable to pay an extra
year's rent at the end of the 7th and 14th years in addition to the

£700 per annum reserved in the lease. The freeholder is liable to pay £1500 to the former owner in 2 years' time in respect of a surface water drain. The current net rack rental value is £1200 per annum. Value the freehold interest.

7 METHODS OF VALUATION

The valuer is often required to calculate the capital and rental values of properties of different tenures and types. There are various methods of valuation that may be used and these will be explained in this chapter.

THE INVESTMENT METHOD

This has been considered in previous chapters and consists of capitalising the net income which a property produces, namely

Net income per annum X Years' Purchase = Capital value

The suitability of the method depends upon a variety of factors, including the use of a realistic yield, an accurate allowance for outgoings and, in the case of leasehold interests, an appropriate tax rate.

THE COMPARISON METHOD

One method of deciding the value of a property is to compare it with similar properties for which transactions have already taken place. This procedure is widely adopted in practice, but requires the keeping of adequate records of transactions.

Professional offices should record all details of property dealings with which they are involved, so that this information is available for future reference. The valuer should keep up-to-date with the property market by reading technical and professional journals.

A comparison method may be used for assessing the rental value of a particular property; the unit of comparison in commercial and industrial property may be the square metre of net floor area and, in agricultural land, the hectare.

A 'zoning' method may be used for obtaining rental values of shops. Shops having the same floor area and condition, and being in the same locality may not have the same rental value. This may be due to varying lengths of frontage. The zoning method takes account of this by assuming that the front area of a shop has greater value than the rear portion.

Example. A shop having a frontage of 8 m and a depth of 14 m has recently been let on full repairing and insuring terms at a rent of £8160 per annum (no premium was paid). Analyse this rent to calculate the annual rental value on full repairing and insuring terms of a similar shop in the same locality, having a frontage of 10 m and a depth of 16 m.

Analysing the rent of £8160 per annum: assume that the depth of the shop is split from the front into two 5 m zones, leaving a balance of 4 m. The value of the second zone is assumed to be 50 per cent of the front zone and the rear zone 50 per cent of the second zone. (It is usual to divide the depth into three zones only.) So that if the rent per square metre of the front zone is assumed to be $£X$, the rental value will be

$$
\begin{aligned}
\text{front zone} \quad &\text{8m} \times \text{5m} \times X &&= 40X \\
\text{second zone} \quad &\text{8m} \times \text{5m} \times 0.5X &&= 20X \\
\text{rear zone} \quad &\text{8m} \times \text{4m} \times 0.25X &&= \underline{8X} \\
& && 68X
\end{aligned}
$$

$$68X = £8160$$

$$X = \frac{8160}{68} = £120/\text{m}^2$$

The annual rental value of the front zone is £120/m^2, the second zone is £60/m^2 and the rear zone is £30/m^2.

Taking the information supplied and adopting the principles used in the analysis, the annual rental value of the second shop will be

$$
\begin{aligned}
\text{front zone} \quad &\text{10m} \times \text{5m} \times £120 &&= £6000 \\
\text{second zone} \quad &\text{10m} \times \text{5m} \times £60 &&= £3000 \\
\text{rear zone} \quad &\text{10m} \times \text{6m} \times £30 &&= \underline{£1800} \\
\text{Annual rental value} \quad & && = £10\,800
\end{aligned}
$$

The comparison method may be used for calculating capital value. Details of a property transaction may be analysed to find the appropriate yield. This may then be applied to the valuation of a similar property.

Example. Freehold office premises having a net floor area of 350 m^2 have recently been sold for £80 275. The existing lease has 10 years unexpired, the net rent being £4000 per annum. Similar properties have recently been let on the same terms at an annual rent of £20/m^2 of net floor area. Analyse this sale and apply the results to value similar premises let for an unexpired term of 21 years at a net rent of £2000 per annum. The net rack rental value is £2500 per annum.

Setting out the value of the recent sale in the recognised way

Unexpired term of lease is 10 years

Rent received per annum	= £4000
YP for 10 years at ? per cent	= ?
	?

Reversion

Net rack rental value per annum = 350m^2 at £20	= £7000
YP in perpetuity deferred 10 years at ? per cent	= ? ?
Capital value	= £80 275

The unknown information is the yields, and these are determined by assuming rates of interest and inserting these in the above analysis calculation until a capital value of £80 275 or thereabouts is obtained. For example, assuming a 1 per cent difference between the 10-year term and the reversion, if the reader chose 7 per cent and 8 per cent, then the calculation would be

Unexpired term of lease is 10 years

Rent received per annum	= £4000
YP for 10 years at 7 per cent	= 7.024
	£28 096

Reversion

Net rack rental value per annum	= £7000
YP in perpetuity deferred 10 years at 8 per cent	= 5.790
	£40 530
Capital value	= £68 626

The capital value in this calculation is too low, so that the true yields are less than 7 per cent and 8 per cent. The process must be repeated, and it will eventually be found that the true yields are 6 per cent and 7 per cent.

Unexpired term of lease is 10 years

Rent received per annum	= £4000
YP for 10 years at 6 per cent	= 7.360
	£29 440

Reversion

Net rack rental value per annum	= £7000
YP in perpetuity deferred 10 years at 7 per cent	= 7.262
	£50 834
Capital value	= £80 274
(say)	£80 275

Applying the results to similar premises, the 6 and 7 per cent yields may be adjusted to $6\frac{1}{2}$ per cent and $7\frac{1}{2}$ per cent to take account of the longer unexpired term. The calculation is

Unexpired term of lease is 21 years

Rent received per annum	= £2000
YP for 21 years at $6\frac{1}{2}$ per cent	= 11.285
	£22 570

Reversion

Net rack rental value per annum	= £2500
YP in perpetuity deferred 21 years at $7\frac{1}{2}$ per cent	= 2.920
	£ 7300
Capital value	= £29 870
(say)	£29 850

The disadvantage of this type of comparison method is the trial-and-error process which is used to determine the appropriate yields.

THE RESIDUAL METHOD

This method may be used to value land that is to be developed or redeveloped. It is essential to ascertain the uses for which planning permission could be obtained, and to prepare an outline scheme for development or redevelopment of the site. There may be a number of alternative schemes, in which case it is necessary to determine which will give the greatest return. The method depends upon making an estimate of the value of the land when developed or improved and deducting from this the costs of construction and site works, architect's and quantity surveyor's fees, legal fees, estate agency and advertising costs, interest on capital borrowed, contingencies and developer's profits. The residue is the value of the site.

Example. Calculate the site value of land which has planning permission for 7000m^2 gross of office space. The development will be completed within 2 years and it is anticipated that rents will be £75/m^2 of net lettable floor area.
Reduce gross area to net lettable floor area — deduct say 20 per cent = 1400m^2

Lettable space 5600m^2 × £75	= £420 000	
YP in perpetuity at 8 per cent	= 12.5	
Gross Development Value	= £5 250 000	

Less		
Site preparation, say	£5000	
Cost of building 7000m^2 × £200/m^2	£1 400 000	
Contingencies, say 10%	£140 500	
Architects and quantity surveyor's fees, say 10% of cost and contingencies	£154 550	
Financing — 2 years at 16% per annum on ½ of £1, 700, 050 = (1.16^2 × 850, 025) − 850 025	£293 258	
Legal costs, advertisement and estate agency fees, say 3 per cent of value	£157 500	
Developer's profit, say 10 per cent of value	£525 000	£2 675 808

Residue　　　　　　　　　　　　　£2 574 192

This residue represents three items — the value of the land; acquisition costs, say 4 per cent of value; and the cost of borrowing for 2 years at 16 per cent per annum on land value and costs

Residue　　　£2 574 192 = $(x + .04 x) \times 1.16^2$,
where　　　x = land value

£2 574 192 = 1.399 x

Site value　=　$\dfrac{2574\ 192}{1.399}$　= £1 840 020

(say)　£1 840 000

Notes

(i) Fees are based on the assumption that professional scales of fees are applied; the developer may, however, employ his own professional staff, who are paid salaries.

(ii) It is assumed that capital would be borrowed for 1 year only at a rate of 16 per cent per annum. Some developers may, however, finance the development with income derived from other schemes, but they would expect some return for the use of this income.

(iii) Contingencies are included to allow for such items as emergencies and increased building costs.

(iv) The rate of profit will vary from developer to developer and from scheme to scheme.

This method is often used by valuers to advise clients on the potential value of their land, but the Lands Tribunal is very reluctant to accept it, because of the many variable factors involved in the calculation. Relatively small differences in approach in individual parts of the valuation can produce considerable variations in the final answer. The Lands Tribunal will only accept the method if there is no more suitable method of valuation available.

A valuer may feel confident in using the method when advising a client as to the amount he can afford to bid when wishing to buy development land. He must be aware of his client's facility for borrowing capital, profit requirements and availability of an organisation for carrying out the development.

THE PROFITS OR ACCOUNTS METHOD

This method of valuation is applicable to special properties such as hotels and public houses, cinemas, theatres and fairgrounds. The value in these cases is wholly or partly dependent on a capacity to earn income on occupation of the property.

The calculation requires the estimation of the average annual gross earnings of the property and the deduction from this figure of the working expenses (excluding rent) and an amount for the occupier's remuneration, including interest on the capital he has 'tied up' in the business. The balance represents the amount available for annual rent, which is then capitalised by an appropriate Years' Purchase to arrive at capital value.

Example. Calculate the value of a 'free' public house (that is, not tied to a brewery) having a bar and catering trade and shortly to be offered on lease.

A typical valuation might be

Receipts from bar and food			£20 000
Less Working expenses and occupier's remuneration		£ 6 500	
Purchases		£10 000	
Interest on capital of £5000 (furniture, fittings and equipment, stock and cash)—allow 8 per cent		£ 400	
			£16 900
	Profits per annum		£ 3 100

Assume that a tenant would be prepared to pay 40 per cent of profit as rent, that is, 40 per cent of £3100 = £1240. Hence

Rent per annum	= £ 1 240
YP in perpetuity at 12 per cent	= 8.334
Capital value	= £10 334
(say)	£10 350

Note Interest on capital—the £5000 employed in the business could have been invested elsewhere at a remunerative rate of interest such as 8 per cent.

This method, used mainly for rating purposes, should be checked by other methods where possible. Comparables may be obtained on the basis of annual rent per cinema seat or hotel bedroom. Valuation of these types of property requires a specialist skill.

THE REINSTATEMENT METHOD

This method requires the estimation of the cost of rebuilding a particular property and adding to it the value of the land on which it stands.

Example. Calculate the value of a house having a gross area of 100 m^2 standing on land having a site value of £10 000.

Cost of reinstatement: 100 m^2 at £200/m^2	= £20 000
Architect's and other fees say 10 per cent	= £2 000
Value of land	= £10 000
Capital value	= £32 000

This method may be used for fire-insurance purposes to calculate the annual premium. It may appear that the premium need only be based on £22 000, because the site would remain even if the property was destroyed. However, it may be practical to insure for the complete value of £32 000. If property is partially destroyed and is 'written off' by an insurance company, there may be demolition costs to be paid. These may be paid by the insurance company because of the £10 000 site value taken into account in the insured sum. For example

Value of building 'written off'	= £22 000
Demolition of remaining portions	= £ 3 000
Insurance paid	= £25 000

THE CONTRACTOR'S METHOD

This method is similar to the reinstatement method, but is applied to those specialised properties such as town halls, colleges, sewage-disposal works and broiler houses that do not normally come on the market. The capital value is found by calculating the cost of building the property and adding to this the value of the site. This method may be used for rating purposes. The capital value is decapitalised to arrive at a reasonable rent, which is then used for determining the gross and rateable values of the property.

The method is difficult to apply to old buildings because there may be unusable and obsolescent parts. In these cases, it is usual to base the capital value on the cost of a substituted building of similar size and using modern building materials. A deduction is then made for age and obsolescence. This allowance varies considerably and provides, in many cases, an inaccurate method of calculation. For rating purposes a percentage of the capital value is taken to represent rent. This has varied from $3\frac{1}{2}$ per cent in the case of universities to 5 per cent in the case of broiler houses.

Example. College buildings, built 100 years ago, are in a dilapidated condition; substituted buildings would cost £1 000 000 to build. Assess a reasonable rent per annum

Capital cost of new building	= £1 000 000
Less Disability allowance on account of age and obsolescence, say 70 per cent	= £ 700 000
Effective capital value	= £ 300 000
Plus Value of land	= £ 50 000
	= £ 350 000
4 per cent	0.04
Reasonable rent per annum	= £ 14 000

The method requires extreme care when assessing allowances for age and the percentages. The Lands Tribunal prefers valuations based on comparables of rentals, but will accept this method if more specific information is not available.

The six methods described above are those most widely used; the valuer must decide which is the most appropriate method to use to arrive at a realistic capital or rental value. In many cases, he may use more than one or a combination of these methods, with one providing a check on another.

QUESTIONS

7.1 *A* is the freeholder of well-positioned office premises let to *B* on a 99-year lease having 70 years unexpired at a rent of £250 per annum. *B* sublet to *C* for 21 years at £1700 per annum, *C* paying rates and being responsible for internal repairs; this sublease has

7 years unexpired. The current net rack rental value is £3000 per annum. *B* has just sold his lease for £21 300. Analyse this sale and apply the results to value *C*'s sublease.

7.2   The head leasehold interest in shop premises sublet for 14 years at £700 per annum net (the sublease has 7 years unexpired) has just been sold for £13 300. The 99-year head lease has 59 years unexpired and the ground rent is £100 per annum. The current net rack rental value is £1500 per annum. Analyse this transaction and apply the results to value a similar but larger freehold shop. This was let 26 years ago on a 50-year internal repairing lease at a rent of £1100 per annum. The tenant has agreed that in 4 years' time he will pay £1500 per annum on the same terms until the end of the lease. The current net rack rental value is £2000 per annum.

8 DISCOUNTED CASH FLOW TECHNIQUES

NET PRESENT VALUE (NPV)

The calculation of Net Present Value (NPV) requires the discounting of all future income and expenditure in an investment situation at a rate of interest, which may be termed a 'target rate'. The NPV is the surplus or deficit which accrues when the immediate and discounted future expenditure is set against the discounted future income. The discounting is achieved by the use of the Present Value of £1 table, explained in chapter 5.

Example. Find the Net Present Value of the following 4 years cash flow using a target rate of 8 per cent.

	End of year 1	2	3	4
Outflow	£14 500			
Inflow		£5000	£6000	£7000

	Discounted Outflow	Discounted Inflow
End of year 1	− £14 500 × .926 = £13 427	
2		+ £5000 × .857 = +£4285
3		+ £6000 × .794 = +£4764
4		+ £7000 × .735 = +£5145
Totals	−£13 427	+£14 194

NPV = £14 194 − £13 427 = + £767

The discount figures in the above are the appropriate Present Values of £1 at 8 per cent.

It can be seen that the NPV is a surplus of £767 when a target rate of 8 per cent is used; this is a profit over and above an 8 per cent return on capital and the return of the outlay.

Assume that the same cash flow is now to be discounted at a target rate of 12 per cent.

	Discounted Outflow	*Discounted Inflow*
End of year 1	− £14 500 × .893 = − £12 948	
2		+ £5000 × .797 = +£3985
3		+ £6000 × .712 = +£4272
4		+ £7000 × .636 = +£4452
Totals	− £12 948	+£12 709

NPV =   − £12 948 + £12 709 = − £239

By the use of the higher target rate, a surplus of £767 has changed into a deficit of £239. A general rule can be stated — the higher the target rate of interest, the lower the NPV.

The calculation of Net Present Values may be used to compare different cash flow situations and to see which gives the highest NPV.

INTERNAL RATE OF RETURN (IRR)

The disadvantage of calculating NPVs to compare different cash flows is that so much depends on the choice of the target rate. The scheme giving the best NPV at a certain target rate may not be the best if the rate is altered. It is better to compare cash flows by calculating the Internal Rate of Return (IRR). This is the discount rate at which the discounted income equates with initial and discounted outlay: i.e. the rate at which the NPV = 0.

If cash flows are compared on this basis, the best situation will be the one with the highest IRR.

In the previous example, at a rate of 8 per cent the NPV is +£767 and at 12 per cent the NPV is –£239. The IRR must lie between 8 and 12 per cent and may be found by similar triangles.

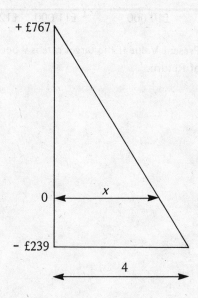

Let the base line of the triangle = difference between the two target rates i.e. 12 – 8 = 4; the height of the triangle = total value of NPVs (ignoring signs); x = IRR – lower rate of interest.

Then $\dfrac{x}{767} = \dfrac{4}{1006}$

$x = \dfrac{4 \times 767}{1006} = 3.05$

$$IRR = 8 + 3.05 = \text{say 11 per cent}$$

The result is slightly inaccurate, because the hypotenuse of the triangle is slightly curved.

An inaccuracy can be reduced by having two target rates which are fairly close together: for example, in the above, 10 and 12 per cent.

QUESTION

8.1   A cash flow has the following outflow/inflow pattern.

	Immediate	End of year 1	2	3	4
Outflow	£36 000				
Inflow		£10 000	£11 000	£12 000	£13 000

Calculate the Net Present Value if the target rate is 9 per cent, and the Internal Rate of Return.

9 INFLATION AND GROWTH

The investment method for valuing freehold and leasehold interests described earlier is limited in handling change in the level of net rental incomes. This change may be due to inflation in the economy which causes the purchasing power of money to deteriorate. The supply and demand for property may, also, change in real terms.

The ability of the net income from property to fluctuate to take account of these factors depends upon whether it is 'fixed' or 'variable'. If income is fixed over a long period of time it is 'inflation-prone'; if, however, it varies according to change it is 'inflation proof' (income receivable under a lease with regular rent reviews may be considered reasonably 'inflation-proofed').

In a traditional valuation, the valuer normally adjusts the remunerative yield for discounting future income and costs to take account of anticipated value change. This might be termed 'initial yield' or 'all risks yield' and is basically net income expressed as a percentage of capital value.

A 'real value' approach may be adopted for valuing incomes in fluctuating circumstances and two other types of yield may be used

   (i)   'equated' yield, which is the true yield on an investment taking into account possible appreciation or depreciation during its life, and
   (ii) 'inflation risk free yield' (IRFY) which can be used to value the income from an investment rising to meet any reduction in the value of the income caused by inflation.

Valuation Methods

Assume that an income currently £5000 per annum, subject to 5 year rent reviews, is to be valued in perpetuity. In earlier chapters, a yield was chosen such as 10 per cent which, supposedly, reflected the possible growth at 5 year periods. The valuation is

Net income per annum		= £5000
YP in perpetuity at 10 per cent		= 10
	Capital value	£50 000

The same situation might be valued with a discounted cash flow allowing for a growth rate of, say, 12 per cent per annum and an equated yield of, say, 18 per cent per annum (about 2 per cent above the yield expected from undated gilt-edged stock, an 'inflation prone' investment). It has been seen earlier that single rate Years' Purchase is a summation of Present Values of £1 so that the valuation may be regarded as table 9.1.

Table 9.1

(1) Years	(2) Income (£)	(3) Amount of £1–12 per cent	(4) Inflated Rent (£) (2 × 3)	(5) YP 5 years at 18 per cent	(6) PV at 18 per cent	(7) YP deferred at 18 per cent (5 × 6)	(8) Present Value (£) (4 × 7)
0 – 5	5000	1.000	5000	3.127	1.000	3.127	15 635
5 – 10	5000	1.762	8810	3.127	0.437	1.366	12 034
10 – 15	5000	3.106	15 530	3.127	0.191	0.597	9271
15 – 20	5000	5.474	27 370	3.127	0.084	0.263	7198
20 – 25	5000	9.646	48 230	3.127	0.036	0.113	5450
25 – 30	5000	17.000	85 000	3.127	0.016	0.050	4250
30 35	5000	29.960	149 800	3.127	0.007	0.022	3295
35 – 40	5000	52.800	264 000	3.127	0.003	0.009	2376
40 onwards	5000	93.051	465 255	13.333*	0.001	0.013	6047

Capital Value		65 556
SAY	£65,550	

* The discounted cash flow has been terminated at 40 years, and the remaining perpetual income capitalised at an initial yield of 7½ per cent (see later explanation).

This approach has produced a capital value of £65 550 as compared with £50 000 from a traditional approach.

The 'real value' approach assumes that current inflation-proofed income will be valued at a yield reflecting real return only, i.e. an inflation risk free yield (IRFY) which may be derived from the formula

$$i = \frac{(1+e)}{(1+g)} - 1$$

where e = equated yield, g = growth rate (as decimals).

Thus, from above calculation,

$$i = \frac{1.18}{1.12} - 1 = 5.36 \text{ per cent}$$

An alternative method to the valuation above using the IRFY assumes that at five year intervals the purchasing power of the original £5000 per annum is restored. The valuation is still undertaken in 5 year bands but £5000 per annum is not adjusted for growth as before. Each £5000 per annum is fixed for 5 years and is inflation prone so that it is capitalised at the equated yield. The capital values obtained are in real terms not monetary terms, so that future capital values should be deferred at an inflation-proofed yield, i.e. IRFY.

Thus the valuation becomes

First 5 years as before			£15 635
5 — 10 years			
Net Income per annum		£5000	
YP for 5 years at 18 per cent	3.127		
PV for 5 years at 5.36 per cent	0.77	2.408	£12 040
10 — 15 years			
Net Income per annum		£5000	
YP for 5 years at 18 per cent	3.127		
PV for 10 years at 5.36 per cent	0.593	1.854	£9 270
and so on into perpetuity			

It can be seen that the capital values are the same for each 5 years (apart from small 'rounding-off' discrepancies) whichever method is adopted.

Both the methods illustrated are cumbersome and a formula has been derived: namely

Income × YP for the review × $\dfrac{\text{YP in perpetuity at '}i\text{' per cent}}{\text{YP for the review period at '}i\text{' per cent}}$ period at 'e' per cent

('*e*' is equated yield, '*i*' is IRFY)
Take the previous example,

£5000 × YP for 5 years at　　　× YP in perpetuity at
　　　　18 per cent　　　　　　　　5.36 per cent
　　　　　　　　　　　　　　　　YP for 5 years at
　　　　　　　　　　　　　　　　5.36 per cent

£5000 × 3.127 × $\dfrac{18.657}{4.291}$

= £67 980

This corresponds with an initial yield of approximately 7½ per cent
(i.e. $\dfrac{\text{Income}}{\text{Capital Value}} = \dfrac{£5000}{£67980}$). This initial yield of 7½ per cent was
used for the reversion in the earlier cash flow calculation.

It is beyond the scope of this book to deal with varying freehold
incomes and leasehold valuations; for further information readers
are referred to the papers of Dr Ernest Wood and Neil Crosby indicated
in the bibliography at the end of this chapter. (Neil Crosby in his
paper proves the two formulas introduced earlier in this chapter, and
also the formula following for constant rent.)

Constant Rent

One of the problems often emerging in the granting of a lease is the
agreement of the landlord and tenant as to an appropriate rent review
period. In the example in this chapter, a 5 year period has been used
with an initial rent of £5000 per annum. If the review period was
altered to 10 years, then the landlord would require an annual rent
which would maintain this equated yield. The calculation of the revised
rent would be

£5000 × $\dfrac{\text{YP for 5 years at '}e\text{'}}{\text{YP for 5 years at '}i\text{'}}$ × $\dfrac{\text{YP for 10 years at '}i\text{'}}{\text{YP for 10 years at '}e\text{'}}$

= £5000 × $\dfrac{\text{YP for 5 years at}}{\text{YP for 5 years at}}$ × $\dfrac{\text{YP for 10 years at}}{\text{YP for 10 years at}}$
　　　　　　　18 per cent　　　　　　5.36 per cent
　　　　　　　5.36 per cent　　　　　18 per cent

$$= £5000 \times \frac{3.127}{4.291} \times \frac{7.593}{4.494}$$

$$= £6,156 \text{ per annum}$$

Bibliography

Articles

Crosby, N., 'The Investment Method of Valuation: A Real Value Approach', *Journal of Valuation*. Summer and Autumn 1983.

Wood, E. Dr, 'Positive Valuations, a Real Value Approach to Property Investments', *Estates Gazette*, vol. 226 (1973).

Tables

Bowcock, P., *Property Valuation Tables*, Macmillan (1978).

Marshall, P., *Donaldsons Investment Tables*, Donaldsons (1979).

Rose, J.J., *Tables of the Constant Rent*, The Freeland Press (1979).

Rose, J.J., *Rose's Property Valuation Tables*, The Freeland Press (1977).

Books

Baum, A. and Mackmin, D., *The Income Approach to Property Valuation*, Routledge & Kegan Paul (1981).

Enever, N., *The Valuation of Property Investments*, Estates Gazette (1981).

ANSWERS TO QUESTIONS

2.1 $i = 0.11$, $n = 1$ year, $I = £750$

$$P = \frac{I}{i \times n}$$

$$= \frac{750}{0.11 \times 1}$$

$$= £6818$$

2.2 $I = P$, $i = 0.09$

$$n = \frac{I}{P \times i}$$

$$= \frac{1}{1 \times 0.09}$$

$$= 11.11 \text{ years}$$

2.3 $P = £250$, $i = 0.095$, $n = 15$ years

$$A = P(1 + i)^n$$

$$= 250 \times 1.095^{15}$$

$$= 250 \times 3.899$$

$$= £975$$

2.4 $A = £1500$, $i = 0.085$, $n = 10$ years

$$P = \frac{A}{(1 + i)^n}$$

$$= \frac{1500}{1.085^{10}}$$

$$= \frac{1500}{2.259}$$

$$= £664$$

2.5

$$A = 3P, \quad n = 9 \text{ years}$$

$$i = \sqrt[n]{\frac{A}{P}} - 1$$

$$= \sqrt[n]{\frac{3P}{P}} - 1$$

$$= \sqrt[9]{3} - 1$$

$$= 1.13 - 1$$

$$= 0.13$$

$$= 13 \text{ per cent}$$

2.6

$$S = \frac{n}{2}(2a + (n-1)d), \quad a = 8, \quad d = -0.25,$$

$$n = \frac{8}{0.25} + 1 = 33$$

$$S = \frac{33}{2}(2 \times 8) + (32 \times -0.25)$$

$$= 16.5 \times (16 - 8)$$

$$= 16.5 \times 8$$

$$= 132$$

2.7

Let the numbers be represented by $a - d$, a, $a + d$, then

$$(a - d) + a + (a + d) = 21$$

$$3a = 21$$

$$a = 7$$

But $a(a - d)(a + d) = 280$

$$a(a^2 - d^2) = 280$$

$$7(7^2 - d^2) = 280$$

$$343 - 7d^2 \quad = 280$$

$$7d^2 \quad = 343 - 280$$

$$d^2 \quad = \frac{63}{7} = 9$$

$$d \quad = \pm 3$$

So that the numbers are 4, 7, 10

2.8 $a = 12, \quad r = -0.5, \quad n = 10$

$$S = \frac{a(1 - r^n)}{1 - r}$$

$$= \frac{12(1 - (-0.5^{10}))}{1 - (-0.5)}$$

$$= \frac{12 \times 1.00097}{1.5}$$

$$= \frac{12.01}{1.5}$$

$$\approx 8$$

2.9 $M = £4000, \quad i = 0.08, \quad n = 30 \text{ years}$

$$P = \frac{M(1 + i)^n i}{(1 + i)^n - 1}$$

$$= \frac{4000 \times 1.08^{30} \times 0.08}{1.08^{30} - 1}$$

$$= \frac{4000 \times 10.05 \times 0.08}{9.05}$$

$$= \frac{3216}{9.05}$$

$$= £355$$

2.10 $P = £400, \quad i = 0.09, \quad n = 35 \text{ years}$

$$M = \frac{P((1 + i)^n - 1)}{(1 + i)^n i}$$

$$= \frac{400 \times (1.09^{35} - 1)}{1.09^{35} \times 0.09}$$

$$= \frac{400 \times (20.37 - 1)}{20.37 \times 0.09}$$

$$= \frac{7748}{1.833}$$

$$= £4227$$

2.11 $D = £35, \quad P = £1000, \quad i = 0.13$

$D = P(1 - i)^n$

$35 = 1000(1 - 0.13)^n$

$$\frac{35}{1000} = 0.87^n$$

$0.87^n = 0.035$

$\log 0.87 \times n = \log 0.035$

$$n = \frac{\log 0.035}{\log 0.87}$$

$$= \frac{\overline{2}.5441}{\overline{1}.9395}$$

$$= \frac{-2 + 0.5441}{-1 + 0.9395}$$

$$= \frac{-1.4559}{-0.0605}$$

$= 24$ years

2.12   For the first 3 years $P = £1200, i = 0.12, n = 3$ years

$D = P(1 - i)^n$

$= 1200 (1 - 0.12)^3$

$= 1200 \times 0.88^3$

$$= 1200 \times 0.6814$$

$$= £817.68$$

For the next 7 years $P = £817.68$, $i = 0.10$, $n = 7$ years

$$D = P (1 - i)^n$$

$$= 817.68 \times (1 - 0.10)^7$$

$$= 817.68 \times 0.9^7$$

$$= 817.68 \times 0.478$$

$$= £390.8$$

CHAPTER 5

5.1

$$A = (1 + i)^n$$

$$= 1.09^{15}$$

$$= 3.64$$

5.2

$$PV = \frac{1}{(1 + i)^n}$$

$$= \frac{1}{1.075^{14}} = \frac{1}{2.752}$$

$$= 0.3633$$

5.3

Net income per annum = £150

YP for 8 years at $8\frac{1}{2}$ per cent

$$YP = \frac{1 - \dfrac{1}{(1 + i)^n}}{i}$$

$$= \frac{1 - \dfrac{1}{1.085^8}}{0.085}$$

$$= \frac{1 - \dfrac{1}{1.92}}{0.085}$$

$$= \frac{0.4792}{0.085} \qquad = \underline{5.63}$$

Capital value = £844

5.4 £250

$$s = \frac{i}{A - 1}$$

$$= \frac{0.06}{1.06^{16} - 1}$$

$$= \frac{0.06}{2.54 - 1}$$

$$= \frac{0.06}{1.54} \qquad = \qquad \frac{0.0389}{£9.725}$$

5.5 Net income per annum = £225

YP in perpetuity
deferred 5 years at
8 per cent =

$$\frac{1}{iA} = \frac{1}{0.08 \times 1.08^5}$$

$$= \frac{1}{0.08 \times 1.469}$$

$$= \frac{1}{0.1175} \qquad = \underline{8.51}$$

Capital value = £1915

5.6   Staircase renewal   £200

PV of £1 for 5 years
at 6 per cent

$$= \frac{1}{(1+i)^n} = \frac{1}{1.06^5}$$

$$= \frac{1}{1.339} \qquad = \underline{0.747}$$

£149

Roof repairs   £500

PV of £1 for 8 years
at 6 per cent

$$= \frac{1}{(1+i)^n} = \frac{1}{1.06^8}$$

$$= \frac{1}{1.593} \qquad = \underline{0.627}$$

£313

Present liability   = £462

5.7 $$YP = \frac{1}{i + s\left(\frac{1}{1-x}\right)}$$

$$= \frac{1}{0.09 + \left(\dfrac{0.03}{1.03^{15} - 1} \times \dfrac{1}{1 - 33/100}\right)}$$

$$= \frac{1}{0.09 + \left(0.0537 \times \dfrac{1}{0.67}\right)}$$

$$= \frac{1}{0.09 + 0.0801}$$

$$= \frac{1}{0.1701}$$

$$= 5.878$$

5.8

Net income per annum = £500

YP for 25 years at 10 per cent and 5 per cent gross (tax 33p in £)

Net interest = Gross × $(1 - x)$

$= 5 \times 0.67 \approx 3\frac{1}{2}$ per cent

$$YP = \frac{1}{i + s\left(\dfrac{1}{1 - x}\right)}$$

$$= \frac{1}{0.10 + \left(\dfrac{0.035}{1.035^{25} - 1} \times \dfrac{1}{0.67}\right)}$$

$$= \frac{1}{0.10 + \left(0.0256 \times \dfrac{1}{0.67}\right)}$$

$$= \frac{1}{0.10 + 0.0382}$$

$$= \frac{1}{0.1382} = \quad\quad \underline{7.236}$$

Capital value = £3618

5.9

$$YP = \frac{1}{i + s\left(\dfrac{1}{1 - x}\right)}$$

$$8 = \frac{1}{i + \left(\dfrac{0.025}{1.025^{32} - 1} \times \dfrac{1}{0.6}\right)}$$

$$8 = \frac{1}{i + \left(0.0207 \times \dfrac{1}{0.6}\right)}$$

$$8 = \frac{1}{i + 0.0345}$$

$$8\,(i + 0.0345) = 1$$

$$i = \frac{1 - (8 \times 0.0345)}{8}$$

$$= \frac{1 - 0.276}{8} = \frac{0.724}{8}$$

$$= 0.09$$

$$= 9 \text{ per cent}$$

5.10 (i) Net income per annum = £750

YP for 19 years at 7 per cent and $2\frac{1}{2}$ per cent net

$$= \frac{1}{i + s} = \frac{1}{0.07 + \dfrac{0.025}{1.025^{19} - 1}}$$

$$= \frac{1}{0.07 + 0.0417} = \frac{1}{0.1117}$$

$$= \qquad\qquad \underline{8.95}$$

Capital value = £6712

(ii) Net income per annum = £750

YP for 19 years at 7 per cent and $2\frac{1}{2}$ per cent net (tax 40p in £)

$$= \frac{1}{i + s\left(\dfrac{1}{1-x}\right)} = \frac{1}{0.07 + \left(0.0417 \times \dfrac{1}{0.6}\right)}$$

$$= \frac{1}{0.07 + 0.0695}$$

$$= \frac{1}{0.1395} \qquad = \underline{7.16}$$

Capital value = £5370

5.11   £12 300 $\times$ $(i + s)$

$$= £12\,300 \times \left(0.08 + \frac{0.025}{1.025^{10} - 1}\right)$$

$$= £12\,300 \times (0.08 + 0.0892)$$

$$= £12\,300 \times 0.1692$$

$$= £2081$$

5.12 Monthly repayment $= 20 \times \dfrac{(i + s)\,100}{12}$

$$= [20 \times \left(0.085 + \frac{0.085}{1.085^{20} - 1}\right) \times 100]/12$$

$$= \frac{20 \times (0.085 + 0.0206) \times 100}{12}$$

$$= \frac{20 \times 0.1056 \times 100}{12}$$

$$= £17.6$$

5.13 Let borrowing amount (in 100 £s) $= x$

$$25 = \frac{x \times (i + s)\,100}{12}$$

$$25 = [x \times \left(0.095 + \frac{0.095}{1.095^{18} - 1}\right) \times 100]/12$$

$$25 = x \times \frac{(0.095 + 0.023) \times 100}{12}$$

$$25 = x \times \frac{0.118 \times 100}{12}$$

$$25 = x \times 0.99$$

$$x = \frac{25}{0.99} = 25.25$$

Hence maximum amount $= £2525$ (that is, 25.25×100)

5.14 Given that the Amount of £1 per annum in 10 years at 10 per cent $= 15.937$ and $(1.10)^9 = 2.358$

Amount of £1 p.a. $= \dfrac{A - 1}{i}$

So that $15.937 = \dfrac{A-1}{0.10}$

A for 10 years at 10 per cent $= (15.937 \times 0.10) + 1$

$= 2.5937$

A for 9 years at 10 per cent $= 2.358$

But A for 19 years at 10 per cent $= A$ for 10 years $\times A$ for 9 years

$= 2.5937 \times 2.358$

$= 6.116$

But PV of £1 $= 1/A$ so that

PV of £1 for 19 years at 10 per cent

$= \dfrac{1}{6.116}$

$= 0.1635$

5.15 Given that the Years' Purchase of a reversion to a perpetuity at 10 per cent after 19 years is 1.635, this is

YP in perpetuity $\times$ PV of £1 in 19 years
at 10 per cent   at 10 per cent

So that $1.635 = \dfrac{1}{i} \times \dfrac{1}{A}$

$1.635 = \dfrac{1}{0.1A}$

$A = \dfrac{1}{0.1635} = 6.116$

A for 19 years at 10 per cent $= 6.116$

A for 20 years at 10 per cent $= A$ for 19 years $\times$
A for 1 year

$= 6.116 \times (1 + i) = 6.116 \times 1.10 = 6.727$

But s for 20 years at 10 per cent $= \dfrac{i}{A-1} = \dfrac{0.10}{6.727-1}$

$$= \dfrac{0.10}{5.727}$$

$$= 0.01746$$

5.16 YP in perpetuity at 10 per cent deferred 24 years is 1.0. This is

YP in perpetuity $\times$ PV of £1 in 24 years at 10 per cent

$$1.0 = \dfrac{1}{i} \times \dfrac{1}{A}$$

$$1.0 = \dfrac{1}{0.1A}$$

So that $\qquad A = 10$

Amount of £1 per annum $= \dfrac{A-1}{i} = \dfrac{10-1}{0.1}$

$$= 90$$

Amount of £1 per annum for 24 years at 10 per cent $= 90$

5.17 Amount of £1 per annum in 6 years at 7 per cent $= 7.153$. This is

$$7.153 = \dfrac{A-1}{i}$$

$$7.153 = \dfrac{A-1}{0.07}$$

$$A = 7.153\,(0.07) + 1 = 1.501$$

Hence the Amount of £1 for 6 years at 7 per cent $= 1.501$ and the Amount of £1 for 5 years at 7 per cent $(1.07)^5$ is given as 1.403 The Amount of £1 for 11 years at 7 per cent

$$= A \text{ for 6 years} \times A \text{ for 5 years}$$

$$= 1.501 \times 1.403$$

$$= 2.106$$

But PV of £1 for 11 years at 7 per cent

$$= \frac{1}{A} = \frac{1}{2.106}$$

$$= 0.4749$$

5.18   PV of £1 in 15 years at 6 per cent = 0.4173

$$A = \frac{1}{PV} = \frac{1}{0.4173} = 2.4$$

Amount of £1 for 15 years at 6 per cent = 2.4, but

$$s = \frac{i}{A-1} = \frac{0.06}{2.4-1} = 0.043$$

Annual Sinking fund to replace £1 in 15 years at 6 per cent = 0.043

5.19 (i) PV of £1 in 47 years at 5 per cent = 0.1, but

$$A = \frac{1}{PV} = \frac{1}{0.1} = 10$$

Amount of £1 for 47 years at 5 per cent = 10, but

$$s = \frac{i}{A-1} = \frac{0.05}{10-1} = 0.0055$$

Annual Sinking fund to produce £1 in 47 years at 5 per cent = 0.0055

(ii) Present Value of £1 p.a. $= \frac{1 - PV}{i}$

$$= \frac{1 - 0.1}{0.05} = 18$$

Present Value of £1 p.a. in 47 years at 5 per cent = 18

5.20 Amount of £1 per annum in 10 years at 4 per cent = 12; s is the reciprocal of this

$$s = \frac{1}{12} = 0.0833$$

Years' Purchase for 10 years at 8 per cent and 4 per cent net (tax 50p in £) =

$$\frac{1}{i + s\left(\dfrac{1}{1-x}\right)}$$

$$= \frac{1}{0.08 + 0.0833\left(\dfrac{1}{1-0.5}\right)}$$

$$= \frac{1}{0.08 + (0.0833 \times 2)} = \frac{1}{0.08 + 0.1666}$$

$$= \frac{1}{0.2466} = 4.055$$

Years' Purchase for 10 years at 8 per cent and 4 per cent net (tax 50p in £) = 4.055

5.21 PV of £1 in 30 years at $5\frac{1}{2}$ per cent = 0.20; but Amount of £1 = 1/PV

$$A \text{ for 30 years at } 5\frac{1}{2} \text{ per cent} = \frac{1}{0.20} = 5$$

$$s = \frac{i}{A-1}$$

So that s for 30 years at $5\frac{1}{2}$ per cent =

$$\frac{0.055}{5-1} = \frac{0.055}{4}$$

$$= 0.0138$$

5.22

PV of £1 in 11 years at 7 per cent = 0.475

Present Value of £1 per annum = $\dfrac{1 - PV}{i}$

So that Present Value of £1 per annum in 11 years at 7 per cent

$$= \frac{1 - 0.475}{0.07} = \frac{0.525}{0.07}$$

$$= 7.5$$

5.23 Years' Purchase in 20 years at $7\frac{3}{4}$ per cent = 10.0

$$10 = \frac{1 - PV}{i}$$

$$10 = \frac{1 - PV}{0.0775}$$

$$PV = 1 - (10 \times 0.0775)$$

$$= 1 - 0.775$$

$$= 0.225$$

PV of £1 in 20 years at $7\frac{3}{4}$ per cent = 0.225

A for 20 years at $7\frac{3}{4}$ per cent $= \dfrac{1}{PV} = \dfrac{1}{0.225}$

$$= 4.444$$

Amount of £1 per annum in 20 years at $7\frac{3}{4}$ per cent

$$= \frac{A - 1}{i} = \frac{4.444 - 1}{0.0775} = \frac{3.444}{0.0775}$$

$$= 44.44$$

5.24 Present Value of £y in 8 years at 10 per cent = x so that PV of £1 in 8 years at 10 per cent = x/y but Amount of £1 is the reciprocal of PV of £1 hence

Amount of £1 in 8 years at 10 per cent $= \dfrac{y}{x}$

Amount of £1 per annum $= \dfrac{A - 1}{i}$

Amount of £1 per annum in 8 years at 10 per cent

$$= \frac{\frac{y}{x} - 1}{0.10}$$

$$= 10 \left(\frac{y}{x} - 1 \right)$$

5.25 £330 represents the capital value of the right to receive £100 per annum for 6 years deferred by a period of 7 years at a 6 per cent return. This may be shown as follows

Net income per annum   £100

Amount of £1 per annum X PV of £1

$$\frac{A-1}{i} \times \frac{1}{A}$$

$$= \frac{1-\dfrac{1}{A}}{i} \text{ which is}$$

YP for 6 years at 6 per cent

$$= 1 - \frac{1}{\dfrac{(1.06)^6}{0.06}} = 1 - \frac{1}{\dfrac{1.418}{0.06}}$$

$$= \frac{1 - 0.705}{0.06} = \frac{0.295}{0.06} = 4.9$$

This YP of 4.9 has then been deferred by multiplying it by the PV of £1; Hence 3.3 is the YP for 6 years deferred 7 years at 6 per cent, that is, 100 X 3.3 = £330, which is Value of £100 per annum for 6 years deferred 7 years at 6 per cent.

5.26 3.337 is the value of the right to receive £1 per annum for 5 years but deferred 4 years at 6 per cent. This could be calculated as follows

YP for 5 years at 6 per cent X PV of £1 for 4 years at 6 per cent

$$= \frac{1 - \dfrac{1}{A} \times \dfrac{1}{A}}{i}$$

$$= \frac{1 - \dfrac{1}{1.06^5} \times \dfrac{1}{1.06^4}}{0.06}$$

$$= \frac{1 - \dfrac{1}{1.338} \times \dfrac{1}{1.2625}}{0.06}$$

$$= \frac{1 - 0.747}{0.06} \times 0.792$$

$$= \frac{0.253 \times 0.792}{0.06} = 3.339$$

(slight difference due to 'rounding off')

5.27   Reduce 4 per cent gross to a net rate

$$4 \times \frac{1 - x}{1}$$

$$= 4 \times \frac{1 - 0.25}{1} = 4 \times 0.75$$

$$= 3 \text{ per cent net}$$

A YP of 10 has been paid for 25 years of income

$$YP = \frac{1}{i + s\left(\frac{1}{1 - x}\right)}$$

$$10 = \frac{1}{i + \left(\frac{0.03}{1.03^{25} - 1} \times \frac{1}{0.75}\right)}$$

$$10 = \frac{1}{i + \left(0.0274 \times \frac{1}{0.75}\right)}$$

$$10 = \frac{1}{i + 0.0365}$$

$$i = \frac{1 - 0.365}{10} = \frac{0.635}{10} = 0.0635$$

$$= 6.35 \text{ per cent}$$

5.28 $$YP = \frac{1}{i + s}$$

So that YP for 31 years at 7 per cent and $2\frac{1}{2}$ per cent

$$= \frac{1}{0.07 + \dfrac{0.025}{1.025^{31} - 1}}$$

$$= \frac{1}{0.07 + 0.0217} = \frac{1}{0.0917}$$

$$= 10.9$$

(i) Allowing for tax on the sinking fund element only

$$YP = \frac{1}{i + s\left(\dfrac{1}{1 - x}\right)}$$

$$= \frac{1}{0.07 + \left(0.0217 \times \dfrac{1}{1 - 0.625}\right)}$$

$$= \frac{1}{0.07 + \left(0.0217 \times \dfrac{1}{0.375}\right)}$$

$$= \frac{1}{0.07 + 0.0578}$$

$$= \frac{1}{0.1278} \qquad = 7.824$$

(ii) Allowing, in addition, for tax on the sinking fund accumulations at $37\frac{1}{2}$p in £, reduce $2\frac{1}{2}$ per cent gross to net interest

$$2\frac{1}{2} \times \frac{1 - x}{1}$$

$$= 2\frac{1}{2} \times \frac{1 - 0.375}{1}$$

$$= 2\frac{1}{2} \times 0.625 = 1.56 \text{ per cent, say, } 1\frac{1}{2} \text{ per cent}$$

Thus

$$YP = \frac{1}{i + s\left(\dfrac{1}{1 - x}\right)}$$

(The tax rate for this x is $62\frac{1}{2}$p in £ as in (i))

$$YP = \frac{1}{0.07 + \left(\dfrac{0.015}{1.015^{31} - 1} \times \dfrac{1}{1 - 0.625}\right)}$$

$$= \frac{1}{0.07 + \left(0.0256 \times \dfrac{1}{0.375}\right)}$$

$$= \frac{1}{0.07 + 0.068}$$

$$= \frac{1}{0.138}$$

$$= 7.246$$

5.29   £1 at the end of each year for 10 years at 10 per cent

$$= \frac{A - 1}{i} = \frac{1.10^{10} - 1}{0.10}$$

$$= \frac{2.594 - 1}{0.10}$$

$$= 15.94$$

If it is assumed that this is left for the next 10 years at 10 per cent it would accumulate to

$$15.94 \times (1 + i)^n$$

$$= 15.94 \times 1.10^{10}$$

$$= 15.94 \times 2.594 = \qquad\qquad 41.35$$

£2 at the end of each year for 10 years at 10 per cent

$$= 2 \times \frac{A - 1}{i}$$

$$= 2 \times 15.94 \text{ (already calculated)} \underline{31.88}$$

$$\text{Result} \quad = \text{£73.23}$$

5.30 Let s = sinking fund for the first 5 years at $2\frac{1}{2}$ per cent. In 5 years, s would accumulate to

$$s \times \frac{A - 1}{i}$$

$$= s \times \frac{1.025^5 - 1}{0.025}$$

$$= s \times 5.256 = 5.256\,s$$

If this accumulates for a further 5 years, it will accumulate to

$$5.256\,s \times (1 + i)^n$$

$$= 5.256\,s \times 1.025^5$$

$$= 5.256\,s \times 1.1314 = 5.946\,s$$

The sinking fund for the next 5 years is $2s$. This will accumulate to

$$2s \times \frac{A-1}{i}$$

$$= 2s \times 5.256 \text{ (as before)} = 10.512\,s$$

The total accumulation is $16.458\,s$ which equals £1000, so that

$$s = \frac{1000}{16.458} = £60.76$$

Annual amount for first 5 years = £60.76

5.31 Let s = sinking fund for the first 5 years at 5 per cent. In 5 years s would accumulate to

$$s \times \frac{A-1}{i}$$

$$= s \times \frac{1.05^5 - 1}{0.05}$$

$$= s \times 5.5256 = 5.5256\,s$$

If this accumulates for a further 5 years, it will accumulate to

$$5.5256\,s \times (1+i)^n$$

$$= 5.5256\,s \times 1.05^5$$

$$= 5.5256\,s \times 1.276 = 7.05\,s$$

The sinking fund for the next 5 years is $2s$. This will accumulate to

$$2s \times \frac{A-1}{i}$$

$$= 2s \times 5.5256 \text{ (as before)} = 11.05\,s$$

The total accumulation is $18.10\,s$ which equals £22 630, so that

$$s = \frac{22\,630}{18.10} = £1250$$

Annual amount for first 5 years = £1250, and for second 5 years = £2500

5.32 Amount of £1 for 9 years at 8 per cent = 2. For 10 years

$$A = 2 \times (1 + i)$$

$$= 2 \times 1.08 = 2.16$$

Sinking fund for 10 years at 8 per cent

$$= \frac{i}{A - 1} = \frac{0.08}{2.16 - 1}$$

$$= \frac{0.08}{1.16}$$

$$= 0.0689$$

Monthly repayment to redeem £5000 in 10 years at 8 per cent =

$$\frac{5000\ (i + s)}{12} = \frac{5000\ (0.08 + 0.0689)}{12}$$

$$= \frac{5000 \times 0.1489}{12}$$

$$= £62.04$$

5.33 Annual sinking fund in 10 years at 6 per cent = 0.07587

Annual repayment to redeem £3000 in 10 years at 6 per cent

$$= 3000\ (i + s)$$

$$= 3000\ (0.06 + 0.07587)$$

$$= 3000 \times 0.13587$$

$$= £407.61$$

Capital outstanding after 9 years = Annual repayment X
YP for unexpired term

$$= 407.61 \times \text{YP for 1 year at 6 per cent}$$

$$= 407.61 \times \frac{1}{i + s} = \frac{1}{0.06 + \dfrac{0.06}{1.06 - 1}}$$

$$= 407.61 \times \frac{1}{0.06 + 1}$$

$$= 407.61 \times \frac{1}{1.06}$$

$$= £384.54$$

CHAPTER 6

6.1 *Freehold interest* Assuming a freehold yield of 10 per cent for the ground rent and 12 per cent for factory premises on rack rental value terms
Unexpired term of lease is 30 years

Ground rent received per annum	= £ 100	
YP for 30 years at 10 per cent	= 9.427	
		£ 943

Reversion

Rack rental value per annum on internal repairing terms	= £1500	
Less External repairs and insurance say 10 per cent of £1500	= £ 150	
Net income per annum	= £1350	
YP in perpetuity deferred 30 years at 12 per cent	= 0.278	
		£ 375
Capital value	= £1318	
(say)	£1300	

Note External repairs and insurance have been expressed as a percentage of the rack rental value on internal repairing terms instead of the normal net rack rental value.

Leasehold interest

Unexpired term of sublease is 6 years

Rent received per annum	= £ 700	
Less Ground rent per annum	= £100	
External repairs and insurance	= £150	£ 250
Net income per annum		£ 450
YP for 6 years at 12 per cent and $2\frac{1}{2}$ per cent net (tax 40p in £)	= 2.625	
		£1181

Reversion

Rack rental value per annum on internal repairing terms		= £1500
Less Outgoings as before		= £ 250
Net income per annum		= £1250

YP for 24 years at 13 per
cent and $2\frac{1}{2}$ per cent net
(tax 40p in £)   = 5.509

PV of £1 in 6 years at
13 per cent   = 0.480

YP for 24 years at 13 per cent and
$2\frac{1}{2}$ per cent net (tax 40p in £)
deferred 6 years   = 2.644

                                                      £3305

                    Capital value   = £4486

                    (say)   £4500

Subleasehold interest

Rack rental value per annum on internal repairing terms		= £1500
Less Rent paid per annum		= £ 700
Profit rent per annum		= £ 800

YP for 6 years at 14 per cent and $2\frac{1}{2}$ per
cent net (tax 40p in £)   = £2.494

                    Capital value   = £1995

                    (say)   £2000

6.2 (i) Assuming that the receipt of rent for 49 years is deemed to be
perpetual and a freehold yield is 10 per cent

Freehold interest

Ground rent per annum	= £ 400
YP in perpetuity at 10 per cent	= 10
Capital value	= £4000

(ii) If the lessees purchase the freehold, the value of the unencumbered interest will be

Assuming a freehold yield of 7 per cent on net rack rental value terms

Net rack rental value per annum	= £ 3000
YP in perpetuity at 7 per cent	= 14.286
Capital value	= £42 858
(say)	£42 850

The lessee would, however, forfeit his leasehold interest having a value calculated as follows

Net rack rental value per annum	= £3000
Less Ground rent per annum	= £ 400
Profit rent per annum	= £2600
YP for 49 years at 8 per cent and $2\frac{1}{2}$ per cent net (tax 40p in £)	= 10.235
Capital value	= £26 611
(say)	£26 600

The lessee could afford to pay £16 250 (£42 850 − £26 600) but he may need to pay only £5000 to outbid other prospective investors.

6.3 *James' Interest* Assuming a freehold yield for a ground rent to be 12 per cent, and that a 65-year term is deemed to be perpetual

Ground rent per annum	= £ 100
YP in perpetuity at 12 per cent	= 8.333
Capital value	= £ 833
(say)	£ 850

John's Interest Assuming a freehold yield on net rack rental value terms to be 8 per cent, adjusted for leasehold to be 9 per cent.

Unexpired term of sublease is 14 years

Rent received per annum	= £ 400

Less Ground rent per annum   = £100

External repairs and
insurance say 15 per
cent of £700   = £105   £ 205

Net income per annum   = £ 195

YP for 14 years at $8\frac{1}{2}$ per cent and
$2\frac{1}{2}$ per cent net (tax 40p in £)   = 5.379

£1049

Reversion

Net rack rental value per annum   = £ 700

Less Rent paid per annum   = £ 100

Net income per annum   = £ 600

YP for 51 years at 9 per
cent and $2\frac{1}{2}$ per cent net
(tax 40p in £)   = 9.388

PV of £1 in 14 years at
9 per cent   = 0.299

YP for 51 years at 9 per cent
and $2\frac{1}{2}$ per cent net (tax 40p in £)
deferred 14 years   = 2.807

£1684

Capital value   = £2733

(say)   £2750

Jane's Interest

Unexpired term of Jill's sublease

Rent received per annum   = £600

Less Rent paid per annum   = £400

Internal repairs say 5
per cent of £700   = £ 35   £435

Net income per annum   = £165

YP for 2 years at $8\frac{1}{2}$ per cent and $2\frac{1}{2}$
per cent net (tax 40p in £)   = 1.101

                                                                £ 182

Reversion

Rack rental value on internal repairing
terms = Net rack rent + external repairs
+ insurance = £700 + £105   = £805

Less Rent paid per annum   = £400

                  Net income per annum   = £405

YP for 12 years at 9 per cent
and $2\frac{1}{2}$ per cent net (tax 40p
in £)   = 4.744

PV of £1 in 2 years at 9
per cent   = 0.842

YP for 12 years at 9 per cent and
$2\frac{1}{2}$ per cent net (tax 40p in £)
deferred 2 years   = 3.994

                                                              £1616

                  Capital value   = £1798

                  (say)   £1800

Jill's Interest

Rack rental value per annum where landlord does
all repairs and insurance = Net rack rent + all
repairs and insurance = £700 + £105 + £35   = £ 840

Less Rent paid per annum   = £ 600

                  Profit rent per annum   = £ 240

YP for 2 years at 10 per cent and $2\frac{1}{2}$ per cent
net (tax 40p in £)   = 1.083

                  Capital value   = £ 260

                  (say)   £ 250

6.4   *Freehold Interest*

Assuming a freehold yield on rack rental value terms to be 7 per cent

Unexpired term of lease is 7 years

Rent received per annum	= £400
YP for 7 years at 6 per cent	= 5.582

$$\text{£2233}$$

Reversion

Net rack rental value per annum	= £1200	
YP in perpetuity deferred 7 years at 7 per cent	= 8.896	£10 675
Capital value	= £12 908	
(say)	£12 900	

Leasehold Interest

Unexpired term of sublease is 3 years

	Rent received per annum	= £700	
Less	Rent paid per annum	= £400	
	External repairs, say 5 per cent of £1200	= £ 60	£460
	Net income per annum	= £ 240	
	YP for 3 years at 7 per cent and $2\frac{1}{2}$ per cent net (tax 40p in £)	= 1.634	

$$\text{£ 392}$$

Reversion

	Net rack rental value per annum	= £1200
Less	Rent paid per annum	= £ 400
	Net income per annum	= £ 800
	YP for 4 years at 8 per cent and $2\frac{1}{2}$ per cent net (tax 40p in £)	= 2.077

PV of £1 in 3 years
at 8 per cent   = 0.794

YP for 4 years at 8 per cent and $2\frac{1}{2}$ per
cent net (tax 40p in £) deferred 3 years   = 1.649

                                                              £1319

                                                              £1711

Less Cost of immediate repairs   = £ 200

                                    Capital value   = £1511

                                    (say)   £1500

Subleasehold Interest

Adjusted rack rental value per annum = Net
rack rental value + external repairs =
£1200 + £60   = £1260

Less Rent paid per annum   = £ 700

                        Profit rent per annum   = £ 560

YP for 3 years at 9 per cent and $2\frac{1}{2}$ per
cent net (tax 40p in £)   = 1.583

                                    Capital value   = £ 886

                                    (say)   £ 900

6.5 Assuming a freehold yield on net rack rental value terms to be 8
per cent

Unexpired term of lease is 16 years

Rent received per annum   = £ 700

YP for 16 years at $7\frac{1}{2}$ per cent   = 9.142

                                                              £6399

Reversion

Net rack rental value per annum   = £1200

YP in perpetuity deferred 16 years
at 8 per cent   = 3.649

                                                              £4379

Plus Premiums   = £ 700

     PV of £1 in 2 years at $7\frac{1}{2}$ per cent   = 0.865

                                   £ 605

                           £ 700

     PV of £1 in 9 years at $7\frac{1}{2}$ per cent   = 0.522   £ 365

Less Surface water drain   £1500   £11 748

     PV of £1 in 2 years at $2\frac{1}{2}$ per cent   = 0.952   £ 1428

                           Capital value   = £10 320

                             (say)   £10 300

CHAPTER 7

7.1 Setting out the valuation of the sale in the recognised way

Sale of B's lease—7 years

    Rent received per annum   = £1700

Less Ground rent per annum   = £250

    External repairs and
insurance say $12\frac{1}{2}$ per
cent of £3000   = £375   £ 625

                Net income per annum   = £1075

    YP for 7 years at ? and $2\frac{1}{2}$ per cent
net (tax 40p in £)   =   ?   ?

Reversion

    Net rack rental value per annum   = £3000

Less Ground rent per annum   = £ 250

                Net income per annum   = £2750

    YP for 63 years at ? and $2\frac{1}{2}$
per cent net (tax 40p in £)   =   ?

    PV of £1 in 7 years at ?   =   ?

YP for 63 years at ? and $2\frac{1}{2}$ per cent
(tax 40p in £) deferred 7 years   =   ?   ?

Capital value   = £21 300

Assuming a 1 per cent difference between the 7-year term and the reversion and following the procedure described in chapter 7, it will be found that the appropriate yields are 7 per cent and 8 per cent.

7 years

Rent received per annum		= £1700
Less Ground rent per annum	= £250	
External repairs and insurance	= £375	£ 625
Net income per annum		= £1075
YP for 7 years at 7 per cent and $2\frac{1}{2}$ per cent net (tax 40p in £)		= 3.438
		£3696

Reversion

Net rack rental value per annum		= £3000
Less Ground rent per annum		= £ 250
Net income per annum		= £2750
YP for 63 years at 8 per cent and $2\frac{1}{2}$ per cent net (tax 40p in £)	= 10.971	
PV of £1 in 7 years at 8 per cent	= 0.583	
YP for 63 years at 8 per cent and $2\frac{1}{2}$ per cent net (tax 40p in £) deferred 7 years	= 6.396	
		£17 589
Capital value		= £21 285
(say)		£21 300

Applying the results to *C*'s sublease. Adjusting the basic yield of 8 per cent to 9 per cent to take account of the short unexpired term, the valuation is

Adjusted rack rental value per annum = Net rack rental value + External repairs and insurance = £3000 + £375	= £3375

Less	Rent paid per annum	= £1700
	Net income per annum	= £1675

YP for 7 years at 9 per cent and $2\frac{1}{2}$ per cent net (tax 40p in £)	= 3.217
Capital value	= £5388
(say)	£5400

7.2   Setting out the valuation of the sale in the recognised way

Sale of head leasehold interest—7 years

Rent received per annum	= £700

Less	Ground rent per annum	= £100
	Net income per annum	= £600

YP for 7 years at ? and $2\frac{1}{2}$ per cent net (tax 40p in £)	= ?

?

Reversion

Net rack rental value per annum	= £1500

Less	Ground rent per annum	= £ 100
	Net income per annum	= £1400

YP for 52 years at ? and $2\frac{1}{2}$ per cent net (tax 40p in £)	= ?
PV of £1 in 7 years at ?	= ?
YP for 52 years at ? and $2\frac{1}{2}$ per cent net (tax 40p in £) deferred 7 years	= ?

?

Capital value	= £13 300

Assuming a 1 per cent difference between the 7-year term and the reversion, and following the procedure described in chapter 7, it will be found that the appropriate yields are $5\frac{1}{2}$ per cent and $6\frac{1}{2}$ per cent.

7 years

Rent received per annum	= £700	
Less Ground rent per annum	= £100	
Net income per annum	= £600	
YP for 7 years at $5\frac{1}{2}$ per cent and $2\frac{1}{2}$ per cent net (tax 40p in £)	= 3.625	
		£2175

Reversion

Net rack rental value per annum	= £1500	
Less Ground rent per annum	= £ 100	
Net income per annum	= £1400	
YP for 52 years at $6\frac{1}{2}$ per cent and $2\frac{1}{2}$ per cent net (tax 40p in £)	= 12.352	
PV of £1 in 7 years at $6\frac{1}{2}$ per cent	= 0.644	
YP for 52 years at $6\frac{1}{2}$ per cent and $2\frac{1}{2}$ per cent net (tax 40p in £) deferred 7 years	= 7.955	£11 137
Capital value		= £13 312
(say)		£13 300

Applying the results to value a freehold interest. Adjust the basic $6\frac{1}{2}$ per cent to 6 per cent for freehold yield on rack rental terms and 5 per cent for the lease period. The calculation is

4 years

Rent received per annum	= £1100	
Less External repairs and insurance say $12\frac{1}{2}$ per cent of £2000	= £ 250	

Net income per annum	= £ 850
YP for 4 years at 5 per cent	= 3.546
	£3014

20 years

Rent received per annum	= £1500
Less Outgoings as before	= £ 250
Net income per annum	= £1250
YP for 20 years at 5 per cent = 12.462	
PV of £1 in 4 years at 5 per cent	= 0.823
YP for 20 years at 5 per cent deferred 4 years	= 10.256
	£12 820

Reversion

Net rack rental value per annum	= £2000	
YP in perpetuity at 6 per cent deferred 24 years	= 4.116	£ 8232
Capital value		= £24 066
(say)		£24 050

CHAPTER 8

8.1 Discounted Inflow

£10 000 × PV of £1 for 1 year at 9 per cent = .917 = £9170
£11 000 × PV of £1 for 2 years at 9 per cent = .842 = £9262
£12 000 × PV of £1 for 3 years at 9 per cent = .772 = £9264
£13 000 × PV of £1 for 4 years at 9 per cent = .708 = £9204
                                                    + £36 900

NPV = £36 900 − £36 000 = + £900

To find IRR, assume target rate of 11 per cent.
Discounted Inflow

£10 000 × PV of £1 for 1 year at 11 per cent = .901 = £9010
£11 000 × PV of £1 for 2 years at 11 per cent = .812 = £8932
£12 000 × PV of £1 for 3 years at 11 per cent = .732 = £8784
£13 000 × PV of £1 for 4 years at 11 per cent = .659 = £8567
                                                     + £35 293

NPV = − £36 000 + £35 293 = − £707

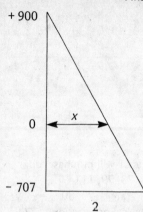

By similar triangles,

$$\frac{x}{900} = \frac{2}{1607}$$

$$x = \frac{1800}{1607} = 1.12$$

IRR = 9 + 1.12 = 10.12 per cent

INDEX